AMERICAN ART & ARTISTS

Series Editor: BRENDA GILCHRIST

FITZ HUGH LANE

FITZ HUGH LANE

JOHN WILMERDING

PRAEGER PUBLISHERS

NEW YORK · WASHINGTON · LONDON

The poem *An "enthusiasm"* by Charles Olson, which appeared in the *Gloucester Daily Times* on October 9, 1965, is here reprinted by permission of the *Gloucester Daily Times*.

For B. R. N. and M. D. W.
with respect and affection

FRONTISPIECE: Robert Cooke, Lane at Age 31, 1835.
Drawing. American Antiquarian Society, Worcester, Mass.

PRAEGER PUBLISHERS
111 Fourth Avenue, New York, N.Y. 10003, U.S.A.
5, Cromwell Place, London S.W.7, England

Published in the United States of America in 1971
by Praeger Publishers, Inc.

© 1971 by John Wilmerding

Library of Congress Catalog Card Number: 75-159501

Printed in the United States of America

CONTENTS

LIST OF ILLUSTRATIONS

FITZ HUGH LANE

I saw the seal of evening on the river.
There was a quiet beauty in the landscape at that hour which my senses
were prepared to appreciate. . . . The
greater stillness, the *serenity* of the air,
its coolness and transparency, the misti-
ness being condensed, are favorable to
thought.

—*Journal of H. D. Thoreau,* 1851

PREFACE

It has been just ten years since I first began work on Fitz Hugh Lane, with these preliminary investigations culminating in the publication in 1964 of my *Fitz Hugh Lane, 1804–1865, American Marine Painter,* by the Essex Institute of Salem. Although a small book, it brought together previously scattered pieces of information on Lane, some already published and much not, and I also attempted a checklist of his works known at that time. Needless to say, what has come to light in the meantime has greatly enlarged our knowledge of both Lane himself and his art.

For example, we now know much more about the chronology and development of his style. Details about his personal life have been disclosed in heretofore buried letters or unculled newspaper articles of the period. Since the first checklist appeared, new pictures or lithographs have been coming to my attention on an almost monthly basis. In 1964 I could account for one hundred thirty-eight paintings and forty-six lithographs (along with perhaps a hundred more probably executed but not located). Today the number of known paintings has been increased by almost fifty and the lithographs by a dozen. Because unknown pictures continue to turn up or change hands on the market so frequently, it seemed futile to attempt another complete checklist of all Lane works at this time. However, since a surprisingly large number are accessible in public places, I am including an appendix listing his paintings, drawings, watercolors, and lithographs so located.

My estimation of Lane a decade ago was based in varying degrees on serious conviction, hopeful optimism, and tentative speculation. It is a pleasure to note that Lane is now firmly and generally viewed as one of the truly pivotal and significant figures of nineteenth-century American art. His work occupies a central place in luminism, a movement we have only recently begun to understand more thoroughly, and his transitional position between the two generations of the Hudson River School has also become much clearer. Incomplete information initially led me to see in his work as a painter, an architect, a draftsman, and a lithographer primarily a picturesque variety; we now have sufficient evidence to discuss convincingly the high quality of his oils and the uniqueness of his personally designed house, as well as the remarkable beauty and strength of his drawings and the original contribution made by his prints.

The enormous expansion of scholarly and popular interest in nineteenth-century American art during the last ten years has, of course, played a crucial role in this new understanding of Lane and his contemporaries. Major museums have mounted large surveys of American art: The Corcoran Gallery, Washington, D.C., displayed its own comprehensive collection in 1965 in conjunction with the publishing of a catalogue of its holdings; the Whitney Museum in New York celebrated the opening of its new building in 1966 with a sweeping loan exhibition of American paintings, including several important nineteenth-century pictures previously ignored; and for its major centennial exhibition in 1970, the Metropolitan Museum of New York displayed a definitive show, "19th Century America."

Critical writing in this field has also been highlighted by new, well-illustrated books, such as Jules Prown's *American Painting from Its Beginnings to the Armory Show*. In addition, the first full studies have begun to appear (in either monographs or exhibitions) on a number of Lane's contemporaries, among them Thomas Cole, Robert Salmon, Frederic Church, Martin Johnson Heade, William Bradford, and John F. Kensett. These studies, particularly, have been helpful in filling in the artistic context in which Lane worked. Now that we are gaining a fuller idea of the individual artists with whom Lane shared similar artistic aspirations, it is possible to make some fruitful comparisons and perhaps see interrelationships among them. To date, American scholarship has largely polarized around either broad surveys of periods and genres or individual monographs. What is called for now are fresh efforts to reach beyond the strict monographic approach to understand an artist's work in relation to what his close contemporaries were doing. One of the misconceptions emerging from much of the writing on Lane is that he was an isolated individual most of his life, that his artistic career was for the most part hermetic. To be sure, his paintings characteristically possess a special detachment and serenity, and as a rule he found his subjects within the relatively confined geographical area of the New England coast. But artists do not grow or create in a vacuum, and Lane was no exception. This book will try to broaden our perspectives on him accordingly.

The earliest serious studies of Lane were undertaken in the 1940's and 1950's. John I. H. Baur, now the Director of the Whitney Museum, wrote the first definitive essay in 1949 on American luminist painting in his introduction to the catalogue of the *Karolik Collection of American Paintings* in the Boston Museum of Fine Arts. The late Alfred Mansfield Brooks, longtime President of the Cape Ann Historical Association in Gloucester, steadfastly collected and catalogued for that museum what is now the largest and finest assemblage of Lane paintings and drawings. At a time when only a handful knew of the Gloucester artist, let alone appreciated the qualities of his work, Alfred Brooks further demonstrated his understanding of Lane by publishing several articles on his paintings and drawings, his house, and the works in his manner by his follower, Mary B. Mellen. Charles D. Childs of Boston was also among the first to recognize the artistic significance of Lane and, through his own thoughtful scholarship and gentle prodding of collectors, helped to bring his art to our attention. Paradoxically, it was a foreigner, the late Maxim Karolik, who put together the second serious and extensive collection of Lane's work, as part of what is probably the most comprehensive body extant of American painting from this period. (The Karolik Collection is now in the Boston Museum.)

More recently, Theodore Stebbins, now of the Yale University Art Gallery, organized in 1966 for the Fogg Museum at Harvard an exhibition of luminist paintings that provided new insights into this aspect of Lane's work. In the same year the DeCordova Museum in Lincoln, Massachusetts, and the Colby College Art Museum in Waterville, Maine, jointly presented the first comprehensive exhibition of Lane's work. It was an especially revealing and appropriate tribute to the artist on the occasion, just then past, of the centenary of his death. Probably the most important recent scholarship devoted to Lane has been that of Barbara Novak in her book *American Painting of the Nineteenth Century*. She has raised some provocative and fascinating ideas about the meaning of measurement in Lane's painting; the self-trained, primitive qualities of some of his work; and his affinities to Emerson, especially with regard to the relationship of the physical and the spiritual in their respective views of nature. Finally, an immeasurable contribution to awakening our interest in Lane has been made by E. Hyde Cox, President of the Cape Ann Historical Association, through whose initiative an unsurpassed collection of some thirty-five Lane paintings and one hundred drawings has been restored, properly framed, and rehung in gracious new quarters at the Gloucester museum.

A large number of individuals and institutions have made my continuing study of Lane both pleasant and rewarding. I am, of course, greatly in debt to the many collectors of Lane's work, who have variously provided me with photographs or information. Their assistance and goodwill have been invaluable. For their encouragement and help I am particularly grateful to Brenda Gilchrist and Nancy Reynolds of Praeger Publishers; Caroline Benham and E. Hyde Cox of the Cape Ann Historical Association, Gloucester; Stillman Hilton of the Sawyer Free Library, Gloucester; Francis Lothrop of the Peabody Museum, Salem; Mr. and Mrs. Philip Lewis; Laura Luckey of the Boston Museum of Fine Arts; Mrs. John Lynch; David McKibbin of the Boston Athenaeum; James A. Nachtwey; Denis R. O'Neill; and Helen Weigle.

Northeast Harbor, Maine
January, 1971

PLATE I. *Gloucester Harbor from Rocky Neck,* 1844. Oil on canvas, 29½ x 41½ inches.
Cape Ann Historical Association, Gloucester, Mass.

PLATE II. *The Fort and Ten Pound Island, Gloucester,* 1848. Oil on canvas, 20 x 30 inches. Newark Museum, Newark, N.J.

CHAPTER ONE
A BOYHOOD TALENT
FOR DRAWING AND PAINTING

Nathaniel Rogers Lane was born in the second house on Middle Street, Gloucester, Massachusetts, west of Dr. Albert S. Garland's, on December 19, 1804. Why his family gave him that name, and why he changed it later to Fitz Hugh, is not known. His ancestors, John and Samuel Lane, were among the first settlers of Gloucester in 1623, and the family name continues today in Lanesville, founded a little later on the north side of Cape Ann. From the beginning, both Gloucester and the Lane family were involved in fishing and the sea.[1]

The future painter's father, Jonathan Dennison Lane, was a sailmaker in Gloucester; his mother was the former Sarah Ring Haskell of West Gloucester, known as Sally.[2] Fitz had one brother, Edward, two years older, and two younger sisters. When Sarah Ann, who was born in 1806, died two years later, her name was given to the next daughter, born in 1809.

As an infant, Lane became paralyzed from what we would now probably diagnose as polio. The Gloucester historian John J. Babson described the incident as follows:

> At the age of eighteen months, while playing in the yard or garden of his father, he ate some of the seeds of the apple-peru; and was so unfortunate as to lose the use of his lower limbs in consequence, owing to late and unskillful treatment.[3]

The artist's nephew Edward gives a similar account:

> When my Uncle Fitz was a child before learning to walk, the nurse left him for a short while alone on the grass one day and he crept toward a bush of Apple Peru and ate some of its leaves which poisoned him, the poison settling in his leg, causing his lameness.[4]

Susan Babson added that "although he grew to the ordinary stature of a man, his legs were useless and he was always obliged to walk with two crutches." [5] Since the apple of Peru is what we now call a tomato, the cause of Lane's incapacitation was obviously more serious than contemporary medical knowledge could tell.

Lane attended the Gloucester Common School but was largely cut off from the pursuits of his friends. When he was twelve his father died, and the family sold the house on Middle Street. They moved into the old Whittemore house, which still stands today on Washington Street next to the entrance to Oak Grove cemetery. John Babson records that "he showed in boyhood a talent for drawing and painting; but received no instruction in the rules till he went to Boston." [6] This was probably because there was little or no training in art available in Gloucester at that time.

Little is known of Lane's youth. Having taught himself the rudiments of painting, as a young man, he was doubtless looking about for suitable local subjects for his pencil, and when he was twenty-six, an event of immediate interest provided the source for his earliest surviving picture (*Ill. 1*). Under the command of Harvey Mackay of Gloucester, the packet ship *Boston* had set sail for Charleston en route to Liverpool with a cargo of cotton. Struck by lightning in a storm at sea on May 26, 1830, she caught fire and sank shortly afterward. "The crew worked like horses and acted like men," stated the ship's journal. First Officer Elias David Knight was one of those who survived, and a sketch he later made of the disaster furnished Lane with the subject for his own dramatic watercolor.

Many years later, Knight recalled the occasion for Joseph Stevens, a close friend of Lane's:

Boston, August 15, 1869

Joseph Stevens, Esq.
Gloucester
Dear Sir:

   Agreeable to your request that I would write something to attach to the picture in your possession of the Burning of the Packet Ship Boston in 1830, your object I suppose is more fully to establish the fact that it is really one of the early productions of our fellow townsman and afterward most distinguished Artist Fitz Hugh Lane.

   The picture was drawn the same year by Mr. Lane from a sketch I made soon after the disaster aided by one of the passengers S. S. Osgood, Esq. afterward a distinguished portrait painter. Mr. Lane had made no pretention [*sic*] of course at this time as an artist and probably had received no instruction.

It affords me great pleasure to present the picture to you who was so devoted to him knowing full well tho' nothing very great of itself [it] would be highly appreciated as the early work of your particular friend.

Very truly yours,
E. D. Knight, First Officer of the Boston at the time of the disaster [7]

The picture itself is painted in pale washes of yellow, orange, and black. Notable are the repetitive curves of the waves, the leaping diagonals of flames and smoke, and the glowing horizon of light—all held together in a relatively flat pattern of great delicacy and striking vividness. The naive vision of the self-trained artist is present here, tending to emphasize each detail as a discrete silhouette and to differentiate forms by clear outlines or changes of color.[8] Present in unsophisticated form is Lane's subsequently characteristic feeling for contrasts of tonal values, accurate draftsmanship, and the drama of light in nature. The work's decorative charm recalls Chinese scroll paintings or Japanese prints; the men in the foreground lifeboats are not unlike those small figures tossing before the great waves in Hokusai's familiar view of Mount Fuji. Lane, of course, did not have such images in mind when he undertook this watercolor. Rather, he shared with the Oriental artists a similar conceptual approach to his subject, and this intuitive sense of linear design would never entirely leave his picturemaking thereafter. See, for example, his early lithographed *View of the Town of Gloucester, Mass.* (*Ill. 5*) or the later scenes, *Salem Harbor, Three Master on the Gloucester Railway,* and *Norman's Woe, Gloucester* (*Plate VI; Ills. 71* and *79*).

During the early 1830's, Lane's talents came to the notice of local lithographers, who presumably saw some of his sketches, and he briefly went to work for Clegg and Dodge on Sea Street. One of the owners, W. E. P. Rogers, was sufficiently impressed to show some of Lane's work to William S. Pendleton, whose Boston firm was the most important of that day. Pendleton promptly offered Lane an apprenticeship. Edward Lane laconically summarized the occasion:

Before he became an artist he worked for a short time making shoes, but after a while, seeing that he could draw pictures better than he could make shoes, he went to Boston and took lessons in drawing and painting and became a marine artist. . . .[9]

Fitz Lane was then twenty-eight. "From that time," Babson said, "his taste and ability were rapidly developed." During the decade of the 1830's he received his only formal instruction, not only from the guidance of Pendleton but also from several other aspiring artists then working in the firm. Gradually, but assuredly, he formed a mature artistic style and soon emerged as a productive and increasingly capable lithographer.

One of those artists who shortly became a colleague in the lithographic firm was Benjamin Champney, and in his later years he set his reminiscences down:

> After a time I left the shoe store, and, through the influence of my friend Cooke, was admitted as an apprentice to Moore, successor to Pendleton, in the lithographic business. Here I was speedily worked in as a draughtsman for ordinary commercial work, the fine work, such as designs of figures and heads from life being done by Cooke. F. H. Lane, afterwards well-known as a marine painter, did most of the views, hotels, etc. He was very accurate in his drawing, understood perspective and naval architecture perfectly, as well as the handling of vessels, and was a good, all-round draughtsman.[10]

Champney's friend Robert Cooke did at this time the first known portrait we have of Lane (*Ill. 2*), who is depicted at thirty-one as a somewhat saddened and introspective figure. He is shown next to his native rocky shores of Gloucester, a lighthouse barely visible in the foggy background, with his legs, the source of his suffering, hidden from view. The ambiguous shadow behind does not tell us whether he is standing or sitting. Helen Mansfield of Gloucester characterized him as a "small, thin man, of the Daniel Webster type of countenance." Another Gloucester contemporary, John Trask, concurred. Lane, he said, was about five feet, four inches tall, and weighed about one hundred and twenty pounds. He further described the artist's temperament as "nervous, quick, and dyspeptic," often prone to moodiness with friends. By contrast, Lane's oldest friend, Joseph Stevens, Jr., wrote of him in only the fondest terms, and John Babson spoke of his "characteristic kindness," adding that he "often contributed a production of his pencil for the promotion of a benevolent enterprise."[11]

Also in this year Lane did a self-portrait, which regrettably disappeared some time ago. (It was owned, and later given to the Sawyer Free Library in Gloucester, by Edward Lane.) It is interesting to compare the artist's features as Cooke sees them—the strong jaw, careful dress, and furrowed brow—with a photograph of him in his last years (*Ill. 85*), in which age has little changed the lines, only deepened and accentuated them.

Cooke, David Claypoole Johnston, and Lane were among the more accomplished lithographers working for Pendleton in those years. Lithography was a relatively recent art, invented in Germany just before the turn of the century. Pendleton employed a number of Europeans in his shop, who helped him develop and adapt the new medium to American needs. By contrast to engraving and etching, which required the digging of lines into a metal surface by a pointed tool or the biting of acid, lithography involved the relatively easy process of drawing with a greasy crayon on stone. The surface of the stone was then moistened with water, so that the greasy ink would adhere only to the drawn parts. With occasional re-inking of the stone, sheets of paper were pressed to the surface to pick up the drawn image. Perhaps the greatest advantage of the new medium was that the lines of the image did not weaken and ultimately break down, as they did with succeeding impressions in engraving and etching, for which the paper had to be pressured into the lines dug on the metal plate to pick up the ink. Lithography thus made possible far larger editions of prints than earlier methods of printmaking, and, as such, it especially suited modern artists interested in illustration, particularly for newspapers, posters, and the commercial arts.

American artists seized on this printmaking method as a unique way of rendering their surroundings quickly and easily. With the advent of Jacksonian Democracy came the urge to celebrate the national landscape and daily activities of the ordinary man. Where the requirements of engraving or etching might have been more time-consuming and painstaking, lithography afforded a freedom and scale of execution that were new. Moreover, Pendleton's shop was rapidly expanding. Its reputation was secure, strengthened by a commission to put on stone Gilbert Stuart's portrait series of the first five Presidents, the so-called Five Kings. In short, the young man from Gloucester could not have begun his apprenticeship at a more propitious moment.

Lane's first dated lithograph done under Pendleton was an 1835 *View of the Old Building at the Corner of Ann Street (Ill. 3)*. His competent rendering of architecture suggests that both his own early practice of drawing and his training at Pendleton's had borne fruit. The view contrasts the medieval gables of the Old Feather Store at the left with the Georgian style of Fanueil Hall, itself embellished with Federal details by Bulfinch, to the right, and the recently constructed Quincy Market by Alexander Parris in the background. Lane has given the foreground narrative interest by including various figures and animals moving across the cobblestone streets. His perspective is convincing, the play of shapes enlivening, and the use of light over the various textures and details well controlled.

Lane's jobs for the most part consisted of executing trade card signs or advertisements—this first lithograph was probably an ad—and music sheet cover illustrations. By 1836 Thomas Moore had succeeded Pendleton as head of the firm, and Lane's lithographs of that year bore the new imprint. Two of his earliest and best music sheet covers were *The Salem Mechanick Light Infantry Quick Step* (*Ill. 4*) and *The Nahant Quadrilles*. Both demonstrated a sure knowledge of the planographic medium, taking advantage of the variety of textures, light effects, and fluidity of drawing that were possible in lithography. The subjects indicated that Lane's attention was never far from his native town on Boston's north shore. *The Salem Quick Step* depicts the local Mechanick Light Infantry encamped on the Salem Common, their tents to the rear. At the left, surmounted by an eagle, is Samuel McIntire's commemorative arch. Although the soldiers appear to be a bit wooden, the print as a whole displays the artist's familiarly crisp draftsmanship and clarity of detail.

Also in 1836, Lane completed a larger and much more ambitious print. He was clearly eager to move beyond the rather confining limits within which he had to work on a music sheet cover. In August, 1835, during a return visit to Gloucester, he conceived of undertaking a panoramic view of the town (*Ill. 5*), to be sold by subscription. The *Gloucester Telegraph* carried occasional announcements about its progress:

> VIEW OF GLOUCESTER. It will be recollected that we stated some time since, that it was the intention of Mr. Fitz H. Lane, an artist belonging to this place, to lithograph a view of Gloucester, provided a sufficient number of copies were subscribed for to warrant the undertaking. The progress of the subscription has been slow, but we are happy to learn it is now large enough to cover the necessary expenses of publication, and that it will be completed and furnished to subscribers as soon as possible. Mr. Lane has been in town during the past week, and has completed his sketch. . . . Taking it all in all, the mirror-like surface and graceful bends of the harbor, studded here and there with the most exquisitely drawn vessels; the lofty hills which nearly encompass the town, and last, our handsomely situated, and really handsome village, forms the most beautiful picture of the kind we ever saw. We trust our citizens, and those who have gone from among us to other places, will duly appreciate the labors of Mr. Lane, and render his sketch not only a source of pleasure, but of profit to him. We would not be without a copy of it, when finished, for five times the amount of the subscription price.[12]

Lane worked on the print through the fall and winter, and the paper reported a note again in December.[13] Completion of the view was announced the following March:

We have received a copy of a lithographic sketch of the town of Gloucester, executed by Mr. Fitz H. Lane of this town. The sketch itself is, we think, most admirably executed; and so far as we are acquainted with the art, there is a softness and beauty in the design, which we do not always find in the works of older and more distinguished artists. . . . We venture to predict that he will one day become distinguished in his art. Subscribers and others may obtain the print at the store of Isaac A. Smith.[14]

During the 1920's, Fred W. Tibbets wrote a long article for the Gloucester paper giving fuller information on the several points of interest in Lane's view:

The picture is taken from the top of Banner Hill, so called East Gloucester, and from a point very near to where the Amos Story house now stands, just off to Mount Pleasant avenue, and the view looks across the harbor and takes in the whole of the harbor part of Gloucester. . . .

In the harbor was one of the Gloucester Surinam ships, for at that time it was almost the hey-dey of the trade which Gloucester had with Surinam, in which some of the old time fortunes of Gloucester were made.

In the distance one can see the steeples of the Universalist, Orthodox, Unitarian and the then First Baptist churches and way to the right of the picture, the steeple of the Methodist church then called the old "Sloop." . . . One can also see the old fort with not a building on it. . . . Five Pound Island is easily seen on the right with but two or three small fish houses. It is an interesting picture, full of much of the life of those days, and one with an imaginative mind can easily fill out the story of the men and the women who then called Gloucester home.[15]

Stylistically, the print owes a debt to the tradition of seventeenth-century Dutch painting, which Lane had an opportunity to see in copies and prints at the annual exhibitions in the Boston Athenaeum. The sweeping horizon and the dramatic contrasts of light and dark seem especially Dutch in manner, although the precise recording of local details and the somewhat primitive handling of certain areas are Lane's own. While we may fault some aspects of the work—the cluttered bird's-eye view, overly flat water surface, or ant-sized figures at the right—we should admire the mutually complementary curving design of shoreline and clouds, which focuses attention on the center of the composition, as well as the alternating patterns of light and shadow that animate the entire design. It was typical of Lane to fill his early views (both lithographs and paintings) with an abundance of narrative content. He was not only interested in capturing the configurations of landscape in and around the town but also fascinated with the incidents and movements taking place in that setting. As the print sold, it of course helped to reinforce Lane's increasing reputation.

CHAPTER TWO
ONE DAY DISTINGUISHED IN HIS ART

Between the publication of his first Gloucester lithograph in 1836 and that of a second one in 1846, Lane was actively at work, first at Pendleton's and later on his own. Except for a few town views, he was busy principally with the production of music sheet covers. One of the most attractive and interesting of these was *Captn. E. G. Austin's Quick Step* of 1837, which showed the Boston Light Infantry marching over a hill in the foreground and what was probably Lane's earliest view of Boston Harbor behind. A more ambitious print done the same year was *The National Lancers with the Reviewing Officers on Boston Common (Ill. 6)*; it presents a sweeping view of the Common with the troops parading before the Governor and his entourage in the foreground. As in the Salem Mechanick and Captain Austin's march music covers, the figures are rather stiff and toylike, but the variety of textures and clarity of detailing lend interest. Lane's feeling for the graphic medium continues to be apparent in his habit of juxtaposing dark and light forms, whether in the row of trees and houses on the horizon, in the branches of the large tree at the left, or in the rows of parading horses. Charles Bulfinch's civic and domestic architecture dominates the skyline; his State House façade is neatly framed on either side by the American flag and the Park Street Church spire.

In 1838 Lane undertook two other city views, quite different from each other in composition and character. On January 14 that year, a fire broke out on the wharves at St. John, New Brunswick, Canada *(Ill. 7)*. Before long the buildings and the docks were ablaze; the flames and smoke dramatically filled the sky with an eerie light, as figures scurried about trying to salvage what they could. It seems unlikely that Lane himself was present, particularly since the lithograph states that he worked from a drawing of William H. Wentworth after an original sketch by Thomas H. Wentworth, an eyewitness. Below the picture an unusually full description of the event is printed, giving some of the details of the damage. The print is notable for the care with which Lane has selected and delineated the myriad details and for the swirling patterns of clouds, partially reminiscent of his 1830 *The Burning of the Packet Ship "Boston"* (*Ill. 1*). The lithograph especially demonstrates Lane's mastery at suggesting varied soft textures, which this method of printmaking was particularly well suited to exploit. Lane also put on stone in 1838 his *View of the City of Washington,* "the metropolis of the United States of America, taken from Arlington House, the Residence of George Washington P. Custis, Esq.," in this instance after a drawing by P. Anderson.

Perhaps the most charming of these early views is the *View of Norwich from the West Side of the River* (*Ill. 8*), done the next year. In contrast to the St. John and Washington prints, this Connecticut scene was "Sketched from nature by Lane," and rather than being printed by Moore's in Boston it was "Lith. and Printed in Colors by Sarony & Major, 117 Fulton St., New York," indicating that Lane's reputation had reached beyond the New England area and that he had now come to the attention of New York establishments. That he was also capable of executing the more than one stone necessary in color lithography seems borne out by the noticeable maturity demonstrated in this print of which only a small number of copies are known. Now Lane's few figures are more convincing, and the receding scale of the buildings more smoothly handled. Many of the houses in the background are a reddish-pink, one of the principal colors in the print and one that would be used by Lane frequently in later views. The total composition is more coherent than earlier efforts, while retaining the artist's delight in engaging details, such as the two cows here at the left or the two railroads (the Norwich and Worcester and the New London, Willimantic, and Palmer) on either bank of the river.

Lane was evidently moving around New England on occasion to make sketches of scenic or interesting locations, because also dating from 1839 are views of *Boston Harbor* and *Millbury Village, Lawrence Quickstep,* and *The New England Guards.* The last mentioned was an illustrated membership certificate for that organization, showing its encampment at Barnstable. The most animated work of this group is *View in Boston Harbour* (*Ill. 9*), "respectfully dedicated to the Tiger Boat Club." Its crowded composition of vessels in the harbor, some cut off at the edges, the glimpse of the State House dome and harbor shoreline in the background, and the alternating bands of light and shadow on the water all suggest that Lane had begun to look at the work of Robert Salmon (*Ill. 24*), the English-born marine painter who had been active in Boston through the decade of the 1830's. The extraordinary variety of sailing craft is enhanced by the addition of a steamboat, a couple of rowboats, and the Tiger crew itself rowing across the foreground.

The one distinct weakness in the print is Lane's handling of the figures, which remain stiff and awkward. Perhaps aware of the problem, he addressed himself to a series of music sheet illustrations between 1840 and 1842, most of which concentrated on single figures, usually framed by an oval or circular vignette.[1] Typical of the group is *The Maniac* (*Ill. 10*), which shows the madman dressed in white and starkly silhouetted against the gloomy prison wall. The figure is articulately drawn; its weight, posture, and gestures are all believable. The mood of Gothic terror and the expressive romanticism suggest that Lane may well have been looking at Washington Allston's painting at this time. The elder artist was one of the patriarchal figures in Boston in these years, and his work was often exhibited at the Athenaeum or at Chester Harding's gallery.[2] Possible prototypes for Lane's lithographs could have been Allston's *Tragic Figure in Chains,* 1800 (Addison Gallery, Andover, Mass.), *Saul and the Witch of Endor,* 1820 (Amherst College, Amherst, Mass.), or *Elijah Being Fed by the Ravens,* 1818 (Museum of Fine Arts, Boston). But whether or not Lane was looking at Allston's work may never be conclusively established; what is clear is that around 1840 Lane's images and style take on a new mood and direction.

The following year he produced one of his most astonishing lithographs, *William H. Harrison, Late President of the United States* (*Ill. 11*), a commemorative memorial. In a pastoral setting the classically robed figure points to the huge stone cross, on which is engraved the deceased's portrait and from whose arms hang scrolls bearing quotations by and about Harrison. Competent enough in its drawing, the work stands as one of the most unusual, even bizarre, in all of Lane's career. At the same time he also continued work on his music sheet illustrations, completing *Mariner's Return.* In 1842, he drew on stone the portrait *John H. W. Hawkins* (*Ill. 12*), one of the few portraits executed in his career. As was sometimes the case, Lane worked from someone else's original, in this instance, "From the original Portrait Painted & Presented to the Washington Total Abstinence Society of Boston by T. M. Burnham." The print contains within its relatively limited subject matter a varied and subtle range of tonalities and textures. It is also a solid and sensitive work of portraiture and demonstrates that Lane was now fully capable of rendering the human figure, even though it was to remain a minor component of his prints and paintings.

Before turning to a discussion of Lane's oil paintings, which he began to essay at this time, a survey of his graphic art and of the development of his lithographic style and technique will serve as a useful introduction to the problems and process of his work in oil. Giving a better idea of the subject matter to which he would increasingly devote himself is the lithograph *Alcohol Rocks* of 1842 (*Ill. 13*), which was also probably published as a music sheet cover, although its format is not quite the same as the others. While its subject is essentially a moral narrative—the vessel flying the pennant "Temperance" sails safely off shore, as the hull wrecked on Alcohol Rocks flies a distress signal labeled "Intemperance"—this aspect seems subordinated to the drama of a stormy seascape. Such emphasis on atmospheric effects anticipates many of his later marine paintings. About the same time Lane also drew on stone an advertisement for *The Fulton Iron Foundry*, which showed a similar new confidence and technical facility in the rendering of architectural forms.

This sureness appears again in the rendering of the remarkable 1844 lithograph, *George W. Simmons' Popular Tailoring Establishment, "Oak Hall"* (*Ill. 14*). The print was one of the first put out under the new imprint of Lane and Scott, an independent firm set up with the collaboration of John W. A. Scott, another young aspiring artist and colleague of Lane's at Moore's. The *"Oak Hall"* lithograph was actually a foldout frontispiece to "a poem in four parts" about the tailoring emporium.[3]

The illustration is fascinating for all the Gothic detailing included, as charming and revealing a portrait of its period as were Henry Sargent's *Tea Party* and *Dinner Party* (both Museum of Fine Arts, Boston) of Federal Boston. Against the balanced design of the shop's interior, Lane sets off the casual arrangement of figures doing business within. Said by Benjamin Champney to have understood perspective "perfectly," Lane here reveals his ability to employ perspective, as technically defined, in a relatively intuitive, if confident, manner. In fact, Lane probably did not use mathematical proportion or single-point perspective to define his architectural forms (as did William Sidney Mount and Thomas Eakins), but relied rather on somewhat more naive and conceptual techniques, such as repeated forms regularly diminishing in scale to suggest receding space. The patterns of the Gothic windows, arches, and vaults create almost an abstract design, providing a distinctive combination of Lane's interests in narrative action and in harmonious compositional organization.

Already in 1841 Lane was listed in the *Boston Almanac* under "Marine Painters" (indicating a turn to new interests), while Scott remained under "Lithographers." As noted, the Gloucester artist had by this time also begun to paint, and a few oils of Boston Harbor date from these years (*Ills. 23* and *25*). For the most part they are small in scale and filled with narrative details not unlike the lithographs of the same dates. Lane continued to work on lithographed advertisements, business trade cards, and the like, although his interests were clearly beginning to shift to full, large-sized town or landscape views, in both prints and oils. Among the last of his trade sheets is the charming *Horticultural Hall* of about 1845 (*Ill. 15*), which possesses all the variety of shapes and textures of his *View of the Old Building at the Corner of Ann Street* (*Ill. 3*), done ten years earlier. But the later work has a greater economy in the total design and a firmer assurance in the drawing of both figures and buildings. Notable now are the subtle modulation of light across the various surfaces and the underlying feelings for abstract patterns in the outlines and details of the buildings.

This ten-year period of active work for Lane culminated in 1846 with the publication of a second lithograph of Gloucester and two related views of New Bedford and Newburyport, Massachusetts. The *Gloucester Telegraph* announced the availability of his *View of Gloucester from Rocky Neck* (*Ill. 16*):

> VIEW OF GLOUCESTER. Our fellow townsman, Mr. Fitz H. Lane, has just published a splendid lithographic view of Gloucester, which we think is far superior to his former one. It is one of the most perfect pictures of the kind we have ever seen, every house and object being distinctly visible. Copies of it can be obtained at Mr. Charles Smith's Bookstore, at the reasonable price of $1.[4]

For an additional fifty cents one could acquire the print hand-colored by the artist. The view in this instance was taken from a large painting of the same subject that Lane had made two years earlier (*Plate I*). Compared to the 1836 view (*Ill. 5*), both now employ a lower vantage point, which emphasizes the lateral panorama of the harbor. The background is more consistent and smooth; the variety of activities depicted is more economically handled. All in all, these latest views have a coherence and legibility missing in Lane's earlier work. In making the lithograph from the painting he made a few changes, notably in the details of the rocks and the arrangement of the figures in the foreground and in the placing of various vessels in the harbor, including the addition of the passenger steamer. While the lithograph was printed in at least two colors and possesses a cool serenity all its own, the oil has a striking quality of strong, clear light, which fills the sky with a brilliant blue and sharply brings out all the details. This concern with light as an expressive element in its own right is one of Lane's earliest formulations of what has since come to be called luminism. The devotion of an increasingly large area of his compositions to effects of light and atmosphere would be a primary feature of luminist painting, in which the glowing ambience of sunlight came to express profound emotional and spiritual feelings about nature.

Lane had a solid reputation as both printmaker and painter by this time, and probably because of the success of his Gloucester views, he undertook two closely related lithographs of Newburyport and New Bedford. New Bedford must have had a particular interest for Lane, since the size and geography of the town, its cultural makeup, and its livelihood of fishing were similar to those of his native Gloucester. He returned at least once again, in the summer of 1857, to record the rendezvous of the New York Yacht Club regatta off the entrance to New Bedford harbor.

As Lane turned increasingly to working in oil, he naturally slacked off in his production of lithographs. As he began to sell his pictures, he no longer needed to rely for income on drawing trade cards, music sheet covers, or other advertisements; instead he could concentrate on landscape and harbor views in oil. In fact, between 1846 and 1850, there are no recorded lithographs. In 1850 he again executed a painting and lithograph closely related to each other, this time of Baltimore as viewed from Federal Hill (*Ills. 17* and *18*). By now he had relocated himself in Gloucester and had begun to travel more frequently along the coast in both directions, despite his incapacitation. Two years earlier, for example, he started what were to be annual summer cruises to the Maine coast; he returned to Boston often, and in 1850 he painted at least two pictures in New York. In all likelihood, he also sailed on a Gloucester vessel to Puerto Rico.

Whereas it is doubtful that Lane visited Washington to do his 1838 lithograph, the Baltimore print unambiguously states that it was "sketched from nature." That is, the outlines of the local topography were sketched in pencil on the spot. Like the Norwich view, it was printed in colors by Sarony & Major of New York. The similarity between oil and lithograph is much closer than the preceding Gloucester pair. The shoreline and harbor view—even the configuration of clouds—are virtually the same in both; only the disposition of foreground figures markedly differs. The predominant colors of both are reddish browns, in contrast to the cooler greens and blues of the Gloucester–New Bedford–Newburyport series. Lane's preference for a diagonally sloping foreground, which appears first in the Norwich view (*Ill. 8*), continues here and recurs again in later paintings (*Ills. 38* and *55*). His noticeable attention to sky in these compositions again anticipates a central characteristic of luminist painting in the following decade.

Without question Lane's finest lithographs were the two he executed in 1855, of Gloucester and, of Castine, Maine, the culmination of long and full familiarity with the graphic medium. His early training and subsequent practice came to maturity in these two prints, done when he was producing some of his most beautiful oils as well. Prompted no doubt by his successful reception as an artist in Gloucester, he lovingly completed his third and final printed view of his native town (*Ill. 19*). By comparing it with his two previous lithographic views (*Ills. 5* and *16*), each done about a decade apart, we can get a clear idea of the maturation of his style and technical ability. In this last view his control of the over-all design and of the placement of critical details is fully refined. His earlier story-telling instincts are now more subdued, and although he is still concerned with accurately recording local topography, he is more interested in rendering the subtler effects of light and atmosphere, as the lowered horizon and less cluttered composition testify. Furthermore, to emphasize the mood of calm and the expansive quality of the scene, he employs a larger and more horizontal format than those in his earlier prints.

A profitable comparison may be drawn between this work and one of *Boston Harbor* done the year before by his friend and colleague, John W. A. Scott (*Ill. 20*). Scott's print shows something of the similarity in style and subject between the two artists and perhaps indicates the influence Lane may have had on the younger man. Since establishing their independent firm in 1844, they had worked closely together in Boston. Moving from Joy's Building in 1845, they operated from 16 Tremont Temple for the next three years, after which Lane returned to Gloucester permanently. Scott stayed on in Boston for several more years before turning to painting landscapes in northern New England, and the two men must have remained in touch, for Lane was active in Boston through the mid-1850's. Scott's *Boston Harbor* is a view Lane painted frequently in the same years, and its composition is like Lane's Gloucester lithograph in the sweeping panorama, crisp delineation of form, and almost microscopic attention to detail. But there is a relative stiffness in the drawing, a hardness in the definition of surfaces, and a dryness in the quality of light that do not match the softer and more fluid effects in Lane's work. Lane had clearly surpassed his colleague by this point: His vessels, for example, sit more believably in the water, and his figures are more articulate and expressive. In Scott's work the viewer's response is dissipated by an indiscriminate inclusion of details, whereas Lane has seen how selectivity in this regard sharpens the effect and gives his picture a focus and mood, with details contributing to the total feeling, not detracting from it. For Lane nature becomes a point of departure rather than a *raison d'être*.

Lane's most accomplished graphic work, *Castine from Hospital Island* (*Ill. 21*), also dates from 1855. Printed in several colors, it was one of his largest plates, and is by far the most poetic and sophisticated of all his lithographs. In it he has caught the steely blue of the Maine summer atmosphere, the quiet charm of one of the state's most picturesque coastal towns, and the sense of love that caressing light can bestow on nature's favored places. What a contrast it makes to his first Gloucester view (*Ill. 5*). Instead of that accumulated activity, Lane now gives us understatement and suggestion. The horizon is even lower than in the Gloucester view of 1855; here the sky fills nearly two-thirds of the composition, and the clouds have an animated pattern of their own that keeps that area of the print from becoming visually inert or monotonous. The lower portion of the design is equally open and spacious. Even less is going on in the foreground, fewer vessels fill the harbor, and the landmarks of the town beyond are sparsely defined. This de-emphasis of topographical detail and anecdotal subject matter is an important clue to the poetic evocation of his later paintings.

Lane cleverly links the near rocks and figures with the far shore by means of the sailboat's mast, crossing the empty water at the center. As in his paintings of this period, he understands and seeks to convey both the physical and the spiritual beauty of nature. Thus this scene reaches beyond the mere description of topography to become a vehicle of contemplation. Such would be the ultimate achievement of Lane's art, and it is to his additional credit that he captured this vision with equal fullness in the very different media of lithography and oil painting. We shall be able to follow the same development in his oils as we have in his prints, from an early narrative style, with generally cluttered and active compositions, to more serene and spacious designs in the later work. What is important to recognize is that not only did he mature as an artist in a parallel way in both media, but his work in the graphic arts provided a firm foundation for all he did later as a painter.

Regrettably, a fire swept along most of Main Street in 1864, destroying much of Gloucester's waterfront, and Lane lost a large number of his prints then on sale at J. S. E. Rogers's printing shop. He had continued with his lithographic work intermittently throughout his later career, and we can only imagine what his late prints may have looked like. We know that he provided an illustration of the *Steam Demi Bark "Antelope,"* taken from one of his paintings for *Nautical Magazine,* in 1855, and the next year he did a lithograph of the pastoral landscape around the battleground at Concord, Massachusetts. John J. Babson called on Lane's graphic expertise when he was writing his *History of Gloucester,* published by Proctor Brothers in 1860; at Babson's invitation he furnished several wood engravings for the book.[5]

Lane's total understanding of the graphic process in his illustrations is always evident. The sense for composing in a range of darks and lights and for working with line and outline would be the fundamental component in the characteristic style that he developed in his paintings. Up to the present, Lane's lithographs have been relatively overlooked (unlike his well-known contemporaries Thomas Cole, William Sidney Mount, and George Caleb Bingham, whose work was engraved by others, Lane made his own prints). They are well worthy of our attention, however, both because they play an important role in his life as a painter and because they are distinctively artistic in their own right.

PLATE III. *New York Harbor,* 1850. Oil on canvas, 36 x 60 inches.
Museum of Fine Arts, Boston; M. and M. Karolik Collection.

PLATE IV. *The Yacht "America" Winning the International Race,* 1851. Oil on canvas, 24¼ x 38¼ inches.
Peabody Museum, Salem, Mass.

CHAPTER THREE
FITZ LANE HAS MOVED
FROM BOSTON

Lane's two earliest oil paintings (both in private collections) date from 1840. One is *Small Cove at Sunset,* which, although unidentified, is probably a view of Cape Ann somewhere near Gloucester. While there is an awkwardness to the drawing and an inconsistency of scale within the picture, the style is characteristically Lane's, especially in its poetic concern with light. His other painting of this year is *The S.S. "Britannia" in Boston Harbor,* which, in composition, is similar to his Boston Harbor lithograph of the same period (*Ill. 9*).

In 1841 Lane's address was given in the *Boston Almanac* as 17 School Street. He must have been sufficiently confident of his painting by this time to exhibit for sale in that year an oil called *Scene at Sea* at the Boston Athenaeum; he submitted *Ship in a Gale* to an exhibition at the Apollo Association in New York the following March. In 1842 he returned to the subject of the *Britannia* (*Ill. 22*) and to one of the favored and recurring subjects of his career: vessels tossing in rough seas. He builds up the paint rather heavily to suggest something of the physical power and action of the scene, and the strong contrast of the dark foreground waves with the bright crests and clouds above reflects his experience as a graphic artist. Perhaps the theme of man isolated before the immensity of the sea struggling through a storm was inspired by Washington Allston's *Rising of a Storm at Sea* of 1804 (Museum of Fine Arts, Boston), which Lane could easily have seen at Chester Harding's Boston gallery in 1839. The image of man dwarfed by nature was a common theme of the Romantic movement in both Europe and America, and Lane's treatment of the theme places him directly in this tradition, linking him with Constable in England, Corot in France, and Friedrich in Germany.

Among the other paintings he completed in 1842 were an oil, *Ships in a Rough Sea* (Collection Mr. and Mrs. Donald T. Hood, Brookline, Mass.), close in feeling to the *Britannia* but much lighter in tonality; and a small watercolor, *Schooner Sailing out of Gloucester Harbor* (Collection Mr. and Mrs. Andrew Wyeth, Cushing, Maine). As we have seen, Lane was working on his lithographs at the same time, and he turned to oils only intermittently, but in 1844 he finished the fine *Gloucester Harbor* (*Plate I*), which he submitted to the "Nineteenth Exhibition of Paintings" at the Boston Athenaeum gallery in 1845, along with *View of the Navy Yard in Charlestown*. The Boston *Daily Advertiser and Patriot* reviewed the exhibition, favorably mentioning Lane's Boston Harbor view:

> No. 87, a fine Sea piece, by Hue, belonging to the Athenaeum must be admired, as a spirited, natural painting. Nor do Mr. Lane's Sea pieces, of which there are two, suffer in a comparison with it. The Marine View in Boston Harbor by him, is remarkably successful. The peculiar effect on the atmosphere of such a storm as he represents is very chillily and naturally given.[1]

The same year Lane painted *The Yacht "Northern Light" in Boston Harbor* (*Ill. 23*), "after a sketch by Robert Salmon," as he indicated on the back of the canvas. Salmon, an English-born painter who had come to Boston in 1828, was the most distinguished marine painter in the area during the period of Lane's apprenticeship. (Thomas Birch was, of course, an equally accomplished and active painter in the Philadelphia and Delaware River area, but there is no concrete evidence that Lane knew his work at this time.) Until his return to Europe in 1842, Salmon spent his entire American career painting within the area of the city and harbor of Boston.[2] His own style was formed in the English tradition that had also fostered his better-known contemporary, J. W. M. Turner, a tradition that drew on the inheritance of seventeenth-century marine painting, with its preference for low horizons and strong atmospheric effects. He was also an heir to the legacy of Canaletto, who had brought to English painting in the middle of the eighteenth century a style of luminous clarity and precision.[3] This latter tendency is particularly evident in Salmon's *Wharves of Boston* (*Ill. 24*), which probably served as a prototype for the later version by Lane (*Ill. 23*). In fact, Lane seems to borrow much from the older artist: the same crispness of detail, alternating play of light and shadow on the sails, bands of light on the water, short, repeated wave crests, principal vessels seen broadside in the center of the painting, figures rowing in the foreground dory, and vessels cropped off at either side of the picture.

Yet there are subtle differences in the two men's styles. Salmon's painting has a quality of action suspended, as in a photograph, whereas Lane's boats are in motion. Salmon's sails are slightly filled, with the aim, one senses, of demonstrating their characteristic shapes; the sails and flags in Lane's painting seem to be actively responding to real wind blowing across the water. Typical of Lane, too, is the relatively distant horizon—the push into space and spaciousness that would subsequently carry him beyond Salmon's more closed and crowded designs.[4] The ties between the two artists were more profound than a common interest in marine subjects or stylistic similarities. Lane's friend at Pendleton's, Benjamin Champney, suggests that Boston's artists at this time were a fairly close-knit group and aware of each other's work: "I [took] a studio with my friend Cooke. . . . At this time there were few artists in Boston. Alvan Fisher and Thomas Doughty were painting landscapes; Salmon marines; and Geo. L. Brown was exhibiting landscapes and marines painted in his early manner."[5]

Moreover, Salmon's lodgings in 1834 (Lane's second year in Boston) were at the rear of Pendleton's shop on Washington Street. Between 1830 and 1833 Salmon did several drawings for Pendleton to be lithographed, including scenes of the Charlestown Navy Yard and the Commercial Tavern, both of which would be subjects for Lane.[6] In all likelihood he met Salmon early in his apprenticeship at Pendleton's and undoubtedly made a careful study of the older painter's work thereafter.

The year 1846 was a particularly busy one for Lane the printmaker, and he did few oils, among them *The Wreck of the Ship "Roma"* (Schweitzer Gallery, New York). He continued to exhibit at the Athenaeum, however, sending a *View of a Steam-Vessel (The Cutter "McLane")* in 1846. The following year he submitted *Marine View* to both the Athenaeum and the American Art-Union in New York. At this time, the New Bedford painter William A. Wall took up residence in Boston and, possibly acquainted with Lane's 1846 lithograph of the town and some of his other work, soon developed a style of painting that would appear to owe some debt to Lane.

On completing the three-lithograph series of Gloucester–New Bedford–Newburyport, Lane actively returned to painting around 1846; in the following year he produced close to a dozen pictures varied in style and subject. Among them is one of only two known paintings he did of historical subjects, *American Privateer Seeking Shelter from a British Frigate* (private collection), a scene from the War of 1812.

Painted probably as a pair of almost the same size and composition were the small views *Boston Harbor* and *On the Wharves, Gloucester Harbor (Ills. 25 and 26)*. Although the Boston view is dated later and signed on the reverse, the writing is not Lane's, and the picture almost certainly dates from 1847. His signature does appear on the bow of the boat, as it does on the barrel head in the right foreground of the Gloucester painting. These pictures record the differing degrees of activity in the two harbors in Lane's day. Aside from the similar configurations of the docks in each view, Lane repeats the spectators looking out at the anchored boats, rowers in the harbor, a dory unloading at the wharf itself, and, in the right corner, barrels, mooring post, and anchor. Certain figures in the Boston view—for instance, the rowers—seem to have been taken out of the earlier Boston lithograph (*Ill. 9*), while the man hauling the log out of the water will reappear in the *Shipwreck on Stage Rocks, Gloucester,* of 1852 (*Ill. 59*). On the whole, the rather stiff and confined composition, as well as its present poor condition, make the Boston view less appealing than the gentle Gloucester scene.[7]

Sometime during the winter of 1847, with his career as a painter firmly underway, Lane decided to return to Gloucester permanently, and in June, 1848, George Saville of Gloucester wrote to his brother-in-law, William E. P. Rogers, in Haverhill that "Fitz Lane has moved from Boston and lives on our street. I stepped into his room after dinner and found him painting a portrait of Eli F. Stacy's little daughter and her little dog by her side. It will be a beautiful thing I think when completed."[8]

Babson noted that "he came back to Gloucester with a reputation fully established."[9] Another unknown friend wrote in the *Winnisimmet Pioneer:*

> We are gratified to learn from some of the leading papers, that the Marine Paintings of Mr. Lane, of Boston, are well known and appreciated. Mr. L. was our playmate and next door neighbor, in early childhood, and we have always felt a strong interest in his welfare. We rejoice that a discerning public has showered upon him that approbation, without which genius must often droop in disappointment.[10]

For a while Lane set up his studio in the western room on the first floor of the old Whittemore house, the one on Washington Street his brother Edward had bought several years before. Lane's nephew could

> well remember during my childhood my Uncle Fitz's "Painting room" as everyone called it. I often went in when a boy to look at his paintings and remember the oval picture he painted on the fireboard that we used to hide the old-fashioned fireplace.
>
> After stopping with my father a few years my uncle Fitz went to live with his sister Sarah, in the house owned at that time by Captain Harvey C. Mackay on Elm Street and for a short time had his studio in that house.[11]

In 1847 and again in 1848 Lane began to paint Gloucester scenes with enthusiasm. Even before relocating in his native town he had completed the little picture *On the Wharves (Ill. 26)*, as well as *Gloucester Harbor* (Cape Ann Historical Association, Gloucester). Many of his paintings of these years show Five Pound and Ten Pound islands, so called because of the purchase price paid by the British to the Indians. At a spot near Gloucester on Cape Ann he painted *Little Good Harbor Beach* (Museum of Art, Rhode Island School of Design, Providence), a picture he exhibited that year at the Boston Athenaeum. Meanwhile he sent to the American Art-Union the paintings *Ipswich Bay* and *Landscape—Rockport Beach*.

The area around Gloucester is, in fact, a lovely one, with its smooth curving beaches and striking promontories. At low tide the large dark rocks stand out boldly, frequently complemented by their reflected silhouettes on the water (see *Ills. 74* and *80*). Not far offshore around Cape Ann lie a number of distinctive ledges and small islands, including Norman's Woe (made famous by Longfellow's poem *The Wreck of the Hesperus*), Salt Island, Brace's Rock, Kettle Island, and Thacher Island, all of which Lane painted at one time or another. About the time that Lane was beginning to paint extensively in the area, Gloucester was becoming popular as a summer resort for both the daily and the seasonal visitor, and throughout the 1850's the Boston papers carried advertisements of its attractions.[12]

Two 1848 views in Gloucester harbor follow the general point of view of his painting the year before (*Ill. 26*), taken from the head of the harbor (*Ill. 27; Plate II*). With his narrative instincts, Lane describes in one the various transactions of fishermen and customers, and in the other the stages of building a boat. Along with these harbor scenes Lane was also working on ship portraits, some on his own initiative and others doubtless on commission. Typical are *Brig "Cadet" in Gloucester Harbor* (Cape Ann Historical Association, Gloucester) and *Ship "Michelangelo"* (Collection Robert D. Congdon, Nantucket, Mass.).

Two contemporary newspaper accounts about his more appealing Gloucester scenes give a good idea of local appreciation for his work at this time. The first is dated August 4, 1849:

PAINTINGS BY FITZ H. LANE, ESQ.—Mr. Lane has now on exhibition at his studio in Elm St., four paintings, one a view in Gloucester Harbor, and the other a composition. To one who is familiar with the scenery represented, an examination of this painting will not fail to impart intense delight, and the stranger to Cape Ann will at once acknowledge that it is the work of an artist who knows well how to transfer to his canvass the beauty which lives in nature. . . .

Mr. Lane's Rooms are open at all hours of the day, and we advise all our readers who have any love of art to call there and look at his paintings.[13]

The second is dated September 22, 1849:

> PAINTINGS BY FITZ H. LANE, ESQ.—Mr. Lane has just completed a third
> picture of the Western Shore of Gloucester Harbor, including the distance from
> "Norman's Woe Rock" to "Half Moon Beach." . . . We advise all our good
> readers who admire works of art, and would see one of the best pictures Mr. Lane
> has ever executed, to call there before it is taken away. . . .
>
> So beautifully is the whole landscape delineated, that the illusion is perfect; and
> the beholder forgets, while gazing, that he is not standing on that old grey ledge
> at "Half Moon Beach," drinking in the loveliness of a real scene.[14]

Along with these various Gloucester views Lane also completed *View in
Boston Harbor* and *New York from Jersey City,* shown at the Art-Union. Although he was active primarily around Gloucester, he continued to travel
farther afield occasionally, and in the winter months he was at work in his old
Boston studio, as Champney tells us:

> That winter [1849] I took a studio in the old Tremont Temple to paint pictures
> from my summer studies. The rooms on the upper floor were occupied mostly by
> artists. Among them were: John Pope, Hanley, and F. H. Lane of old lithographic
> days, and now a marine painter.[15]

Lane was moving about to secure new subjects, and his art was also gaining
wider exposure. Primarily through the appearance of his work at the American
Art-Union in New York, his reputation was beginning to reach beyond his
home town. His great friend from Gloucester, Joseph L. Stevens, Jr., was partly
responsible, in his capacity as local secretary for the Art-Union. On June 4, 1849
he reported to the Gloucester paper:

> AMERICAN ART-UNION.—We are indebted to Mr. Joseph L. Stevens Jr.,
> secretary of the American Art-Union for this town, and vicinity, for copies of the
> "Transactions," for 1848, and the April number of the monthly Bulletin of this
> Association. . . .
>
> Among the landscape paintings distributed, we find in the catalogue two by
> Fitz H. Lane Esq. of this town, viz. "Rockport Beach" and "Ipswich Bay." [16]

It was also owing to Stevens that Lane visited Maine; during the summer of
1848, the painter made his first recorded trip there. From this experience, he
painted *View on the Penobscot* and *Twilight on the Kennebec* (*Ill. 35*) the
next winter, pictures he also placed on exhibition at the Art-Union. The latter,
especially, was to be a pivotal work both for himself and for many of his
colleagues.

CHAPTER FOUR
A COMMANDING VIEW
OF THE HARBOR

The decade of the 1850's was for Lane one of prodigious work. Most important, it saw him develop and perfect a mature style and personal vision that he carried to his last works. He was also active in Gloucester's civic affairs and in the building of his own house (*Ill. 28*), which turned out to be an uncommon reflection of his personality as a man and an artist. He had bought a piece of rising land on Duncan Street, near the water, sometime in 1849 and negotiated easements with his neighbors, Frederick G. Low and William Babson.[1] With his brother-in-law, Ignatius Winter, he immediately began designing and then constructing a seven-gable house of granite. Lane chose as a site the top of Duncan's Point (later known as Ivy Court), which afforded a sweeping view of the town and harbor, as shown in one of his drawings looking toward the house from the water (*Ill. 29*). In addition, local history held that on this site "the beacons were lighted that celebrated the news of the Declaration of Independence in 1776."[2] Curiously enough, it is said to be one of only seven granite houses on Cape Ann, even though that stone is relatively common in New England. Lane and the Winters moved in shortly after New Year's, 1850.

The inspiration for the design came from the well-known House of Seven Gables made popular by Hawthorne's romantic tale. Its tall, narrow proportions and massive stonework were in keeping with the then fashionable revival of medieval styles in architecture. But they also clearly reflected Lane's Romantic sensibility: for here he created a solid fortress in the Gothic spirit to serve both as a rough outcropping of nature and as a secure bulwark against her temperamental forces. The picturesque isolation of the house was surely an extension of his own quiet loneliness and his contemplative attitude toward the natural world. No less than his most poetic paintings, it gives a revealing insight into his introspective personality. While the exterior forms and details allude more directly to the medieval styles of seventeenth- and early eighteenth-century American architecture, the inside displays an unusual arrangement of Gothic vaults, derived, of course, from mid-nineteenth-century revival examples (*see Ill. 14*). There are a full basement and two main floors; the few rooms are large and high-ceilinged, although the passageways and staircases are dark and narrow. Because there are seven gables, the corresponding vaults beneath face each other asymmetrically and bear little relation to the walls of the rooms.

The large windows, accentuated outside by the thick slabs of granite, provided Lane ample opportunity for observing points of interest and also flooded his second-floor studio with light. Fred W. Tibbets, a local commentator, later recalled that, "as originally built by Mr. Lane, the studio had a large glass roof for getting the right light for painting. The gardens were beautifully laid out." [3]

Others remembered paying cautious visits to watch the artist at work. Charles Sawyer, for example,

> said that as a boy about four or five years old, he used to come over with his mother to spend the summer months with his grandfather while his father went to the Bay mackerelling, for he was of the Eastern Point Sawyers. And he well remembers playing with Jimmie Winter, who was the son of Mr. and Mrs. Ignatius Winter, the mother being the sister of Fitz Lane and kept house for him in the stone house on Ivy court. Jimmy Winter was about the age of young Sawyer and many was the time that they two would creep into the studio of Mr. Lane and watch him at work upon his pictures.[4]

Susan Babson also noted that

> Many of his pictures were painted from his studio whose windows commanded a view of the harbor and bits of the coast. . . .
>
> Several people are still living who remember him and his peculiar personality. . . . Mrs. Charles Rogers . . . remembers being taken by her mother as a little girl to see his wonderful garden laid out in terraces and cared for by himself—she remembers especially very large balsams that resembled roses.[5]

Following Lane's death in 1865, Captain Frederick G. Low, the owner of a large neighboring estate, bought the Lane property and lived in the house himself for a number of years. Later it served for a time as a jail, and it is still known by some as the Old Stone Jug. During the 1960's the town of Gloucester undertook a waterfront renewal project, turning Duncan's Point into a park, and the land around the house again began to look as it might have in Lane's day—a fitting memorial to one of Gloucester's most distinguished sons.

Lane meanwhile was involved in local events, organizing and participating in a Fourth of July celebration, probably in the 1850's, among other things. His contributions were not in his usual line, as the Gloucester paper described the occasion:

After [a floral display] came the Chief Marshal of the Floral procession, Mr. J. J. Piper, accompanied by F. H. Lane, Esq. in an open carriage. To these gentlemen succeeded [sic] the Banner of the procession, which was carried as were all the other banners, by boys who were evidently wide awake. And under what more appropriate Sign could we marshal our children than the portrait of the Patriot and Hero whose fame and whose memory are their pride? Encircled by a garland of Oak leaves the cherished features of Washington were surrounded by the motto "First in war, first in peace, and first in the hearts of his countrymen." This banner was surmounted by an Eagle, so perfectly designed and executed that we supposed it to be one of those proud birds which have been recently hovering o'er the Cape, perched upon the banner, until we were informed that it was the production of Mr. Lane assisted by a lady who is ever zealous in good works. . . .

To F. H. Lane Esq. whose Skill as an artist is so well known and appreciated, the Floral procession was indebted for much of its beauty, especially for the banners and paintings; his whole time for several days having been devoted with his usual liberality to the success of the undertaking.

At the end of the article the organizers appended their own note:

ACKNOWLEDGMENT. The undersigned, managers of the Floral Procession on the Fourth, would render their earnest thanks to the ladies who undertook with so much zeal and perseverance to prepare the schools for the occasion. The complete success which attended this undertaking, novel here and difficult to accomplish in so short a time, is wholly attributable to the promptness with which they accepted and carried out our hasty designs. While they will feel amply repaid for their laborious exertions, by the success of the undertaking, and the pleasure it has afforded to so many of our young friends, we shall remember their kind assistance as a pleasing token of approbation.

JOHN J. PIPER.
FITZ H. LANE.[6]

Lane's work as a maker of banners and signs is virtually unknown, and unfortunately none of his efforts for this Fourth of July parade are extant. But he did paint other signs, and one oil painting commissioned as a sign that he did for a Gloucester shipbuilder in 1857 (Ill. 71) has survived.

In the same year that he moved into his new house, 1850, he painted several local scenes as well as a number elsewhere. One of his favorite views in Gloucester was that of the harbor shown in *The Old Fort and Ten Pound Island* (*Ill. 30*), a slight variation on his 1848 and 1849 versions of the subject (see *Ill. 27*). The later painting is particularly interesting because Lane's finished oil study also survives (*Ill. 31*) and may be compared with the final picture. Together they tell us something about his method of working. He generally started outdoors with pencil drawings, then blocked out the major forms in oil on a small canvas in the studio. The contours in the study were at this point clearly defined, with special attention to patterns and placement of light and dark shapes. In the larger scale of the final work, he punctuated the generalized structural underpainting, adding vessels in the harbor and clouds in the sky. For all the realism of these details, indicating study from life, their judicious placement across the canvas is just as clearly not a reflection of any natural configuration, but the product of Lane's artistic sensibility—a controlled selectivity in the service of the pictorial statement. The vessels stand almost like musical notations, with rhythmic intervals between them, while each is the counterpoint to some rock or building nearby. Similarly, the cloud formations above reach out like enclosing arms over the scene to complement the curving lines of the shore and the balanced land masses at either side of the composition.

It appears that 1850 was also a year of extensive travel for Lane. In that year he visited New York and painted several views of the harbor, one of which he exhibited at the Art-Union. One of his largest paintings done there, the superb *New York Harbor (Plate III)*, is composed in a manner similar to earlier views of Boston (see *Ills. 23* and *25*), although it is more complex than any of the previous views. Lane balances asymmetrically two pyramidal groups of vessels on either side of the picture and introduces a subtle play of alternately dark and light hulls, as well as contrasting sail patterns. All in all, it is a stunning display of beautifully wrought details combined with grandeur of design.

It is less certain that Lane painted *St. John's, Porto Rico (Ill. 32)* on the site, although the particulars of the setting are so accurate that it is conceivable he based his work on firsthand observations. Along with two New York views, this picture belonged to Sidney Mason, a Gloucester native who had business interests in Puerto Rico. (The men in the foreground of the painting are said to be logging mahogany floated from the Mason plantation.) [7] Lane knew the Mason family well; he gave painting lessons to Mason's daughter Harriet and in 1849 presented her with a still life he had painted (*Ill. 33*; the still life remains in the family today, an exquisite spray of flowers delicately drawn and colored against a neutral background. It is the only known still life by Lane extant.) Although not a confirmed fact, it is entirely possible that Lane voyaged to Puerto Rico on a Mason ship.

Gloucester was not only the oldest fishing port in America, but in the middle of the nineteenth century it also saw extensive activity in trade to and from Surinam (alternatively known as Dutch Guiana), on the north coast of South America, activity that did not escape Lane's notice. About 1850, for example, he painted *Surinam Brig in Rough Seas* (Marblehead Historical Society, Marblehead, Mass.) and in 1852 the watercolor *Brig "Agenosa" Laying* [*sic*] *in Gloucester Harbor—Bound for Surinam* (Cape Ann Historical Association, Gloucester).

In any event, Lane did get as far as Baltimore that year, where he painted *Baltimore from Federal Hill* (*Ill. 17*) and *Baltimore Harbor* (Arpad Gallery, Washington, D.C.). Back home, he continued his painting of ship portraits, completing paired views of the *Loo Choo* in calm and in rough waters. At the same time he undertook his second historical work, *The U.S. Frigate "President" Engaging the British Squadron, 1815* (Corcoran Gallery, Washington, D.C.). Gloucester scenes continued to occupy him, notably oils of vessels tossing on rough seas or sailing near rocky leeward shores along Cape Ann. One Gloucester harbor view in particular (The Mariners Museum, Newport News, Va.) is unusually Dutch in feeling, with its low horizon, strong narrative content, and vaporous atmospheric effects.

Local critical comment about Lane's work remained appreciative:

> PAINTINGS. Two fine views of Gloucester Beach, from Fort Point and Canal Rocks, by Fitz W. [*sic*] Lane, Esq., may be seen at the artist's rooms. They are not surpassed in beauty of finish by any of Lane's productions, and the accuracy with which every object in the vicinity of the beach is delineated, will render them particularly interesting to the citizens of Gloucester and those familiar with its scenery.[8]

At the 1850 Athenaeum exhibition he showed a *Marine View,* and in the same catalogue Allston's *Moonlit Landscape* (Boston Museum) was also listed, indicating another opportunity for Lane to see the older artist's work. In fact, much of Allston's lyrical nostalgia seems to have been reborn in Lane's tranquil designs; not long afterward, he began a series of his own moonlight scenes (*Ill. 62*), which suggest a definite debt to the combination of Romantic emotion and classical restraint in Allston's work. Another article in the Gloucester newspaper on October 23, 1850, described further local pictures:

> GOOD HARBOR BEACH.—Fitz H. Lane, Esq., has just finished a view of

Good Harbor Beach; and if we are not mistaken, it will be pronounced as fine a painting as the artist has ever produced. . . .

As a place to dream in, a refuge from the drudgery of our employment, endeared by the remembrance of pleasant converse with friends, we and not a few of our readers will consider "Bass Rocks" unrivalled by any of the wild and beautiful localities so common to Cape Ann.[9]

Meanwhile, the Boston papers continued to receive favorable pieces of information on Lane from the Art-Union:

AMERICAN ART-UNION. The first number of the Bulletin of the American Art-Union for 1850 has reached our hands, and we are glad to see it has assumed a permanent shape and gives promise of a real benefit to the cause of art. . . .

Prefixed is a list of the pictures already purchased for distribution at the annual meeting: among them we notice pictures by Doughty, Birch, Weir, Hubbard, Gerry, Lane, and others of less repute.[10]

But perhaps the most revealing notice to appear was a review of pictures from the Düsseldorf School on exhibit in New York. After commenting on the show, which offered works by Hubner, Leutze, and Achenbach—all popular and respected names—the writer went on to compare them to the American collection hung at the Art-Union:

THE DUSSELDORF PAINTINGS.—New York, May 8, 1850. Let no lover of art who may visit New York omit seeing the collection of paintings by artists of the Dusseldorf Academy, now on exhibition in the hall over the vestibule of the New Mr. Bellow's church, Broadway. It comprises upwards of a hundred productions in various styles of art, but all of rare merit and extraordinary finish. . . . Passing from this superb collection into the hall of the Art-Union, a few blocks farther down Broadway, the contrast was by no means agreeable. You felt the pressure of a different atmosphere. It was a transition from the mature and perfect to the unripe and rudimental. And yet there are a few good pictures, among many abominations, on the walls of the Art-Union. [Thomas] Hinckley has contributed one of his fine cattle-pieces; and Lane a harbor scene, very good, but inferior to many of his marine views owned in Boston. The farther Lane gets out to sea the more at home he seems to be. There is nothing in the Dusseldorf collection, in the way of marine views, that can be called equal to the best of Lane's. His ships in a squall, his sketches of Cape Ann seaside scenery, and all his salt-water and boating scenes are unequalled in their fidelity to the ocean's varying aspects. For the information of those, who are not familiar with the merits of this artist, I would say, he is a resident of Gloucester, Massachusetts, where nautical subjects have been his study from a boy, and that he deserves to be better known.[11]

The start of the America's Cup competition in 1851 naturally drew the attention of marine painters, among them Lane and James E. Buttersworth.[12] Lane painted at least two pictures of the yacht *America*. One shows her winning the first international race (*Plate IV*), a scene that Lane atypically based on a lithograph by Thomas Dutton. It is a painting of bright color and lively interest. The drawing throughout is crisp, and all the craft are sharply defined, none more so than the graceful *America* herself in the foreground. Although Lane has placed her at the center of the painting, he creates diversionary points of attention with the other sailing boats to the left and passenger vessels on the right. A second, smaller oil (Samuel L. Lowe, Jr., Antiques, Inc., Boston) shows the yacht three times, sequentially seen from different points of view as she is rounding a mark.

Other ship portraits engaged Lane's attention during the early 1850's, which he handled with varying success. One of his strongest from 1851 is the *Ship "Southern Cross" in Boston Harbor* (Collection Stephen Wheatland, Brookline, Mass.), and a more perfunctory oil done at the same time shows the *Samuel Lawrence* (Peabody Museum, Salem, Mass.), sailing with other vessels nearby. Despite his still uneven performance, however, the Boston *Transcript* concluded, "Since Salmon's death, we have no one who can paint a ship and ocean prospect like [Lane]. His 'squalls at sea' are the best things of the kind that we remember to have seen." [13]

Not surprisingly, the newly founded but short-lived New England Art Union mentioned Lane's work favorably:

> The Art Union now has some excellent paintings on exhibition at its room. Among them we notice . . . a view of Gloucester harbor by Lane.
> The New England Art Union is now fairly launched upon the tide of popular favor. . . . We commend the institution to public support; and hope that its prosperity will be equal to its claims.[14]

Boston, regrettably, could not support its own Art Union, and the institution closed after a year of business. Of minor interest was the fact that Lane's address was given as Tremont Temple, which suggests that he was still spending some time at work in Boston during the winter months. He was probably moving around for subject matter, and he was also trying his hand at subjects more varied than at any other time in his career. One unusual work is among the very few portraits of individuals by Lane still extant: *Captain John Somes* (Collection William Webber, Jr., Gloucester, Mass.), copied after an original pastel by Benjamin Blyth in the Cape Ann Historical Association. On the back of his canvas Lane inscribed, "Copied from the Original, in the possession of Mrs. Collins, by Fitz H. Lane, Septr. 1851."

During the fall and spring months Lane spent much of his time making pencil sketches around Gloucester, and from his surviving drawings it is apparent that he knew intimately the details of almost the entire Cape Ann shoreline. Between 1850 and his death in 1865 he made drawings of every prominent point and cove, offshore island or intown building. Sometimes he did several sketches of the same spot, changing his viewpoint slightly or moving in for a closer look at some detail. Typical are two delicate drawings of the Pavillion Hotel fronting Gloucester's main beach (Cape Ann Historical Association, Gloucester). The drawings view the hotel from the two ends of the beach; one, *Gloucester Beach from the Cut* served as a preliminary study for a larger oil (Collection Nina Fletcher Little, Brookline, Mass.), in which the scene is bathed in the cool pink rays of dawn.

In fact, the romantic drama of time's transitional moments was increasingly appealing to Lane. His natural absorption with the rendering of effects of light and atmosphere led him more and more often to attempt pictures of sunrise and sunset. As the true subjects of his paintings, consequently, became primarily time and mood, his attention to narrative details slackened.

One picture in the new vein is the small oil on panel called *Ten Pound Island at Sunset* (*Ill. 34*), signed on the reverse "Composition, F. H. Lane to J. L. Stevens, Jr., 1851." Two small sailboats drift in the dark shadows near the island, as the incandescent glow of sunset fills the distant horizon. The design of the painting is simple and quiet, appropriate to the subject, and the depersonalized figures, which we see only from the back, contribute to the mood of dreamy contemplation before nature. An additional fact of interest is a second signature on the back: "D. Jerome Elwell touched upon, March 13, '91." Elwell was a younger admirer of Lane's and later painted in his manner (see *Ill. 83*); he also "strengthened" (so he must have thought) a number of Lane's typically understated works. But *Ten Pound Island,* now cleaned and restored to its original tonalities, is a revealing barometer of Lane's changing sensibility. The new elements at this time were his friendship with Joseph Stevens, his increasing preference for scenes of dawn and dusk, and his marked use of hotter colors to render those special effects. The experience of Maine proved to be the catalyst that brought together these ingredients.

CHAPTER FIVE
THE MEANING OF MAINE

At the Art-Union exhibition of 1849 Lane was represented by four pictures, *View in Boston Harbor, New York from Jersey City, View on the Penobscot,* and *Twilight on the Kennebec* (*Ill. 35*). This last was lent by W. H. Wheeler of Lynn and was described in the catalogue as follows: "The western sky is still glowing in the rays of the setting sun. In the foreground is a vessel lying in the shadow. The river stretches across the picture." [1]

From the top of the painting a deep blue sky fades into pale pink and yellow at the horizon, starkly silhouetting the weathered northern pines. Virtually without figures, the picture intimates humanity only in the grounded vessel; otherwise, it is an image of pure nature, of raw wilderness. Lane must have been struck by the distinctive tranquility as well as by the natural drama before his eyes. Here was a direct confrontation with nature and time, almost devoid of man's civilizing influences. Lane and other American artists were in search of a pristine wilderness in which they might realize their image of a growing national consciousness. The popularity of Niagara Falls since the eighteenth century, later of the White Mountains and the Hudson River, then of the Rocky Mountains and the American West, and finally of South America and the Arctic, gave continuing evidence that Americans truly believed the virtues and youthfulness of their country superior to the age and corruptions of Europe. Part of this new vision was a response to the enthusiasms of Jacksonian Democracy, which inspired in Americans a rising sense of national self-confidence. Places of wild or scenic beauty therefore became symbols of youthful, native power. These attitudes also emerged in the thought and literature of the period: Thoreau and Emerson celebrated man's harmony with nature, at the same time consecrating nature with a mantle of divinity. Thus the American wilderness came to be viewed as a manifestation of God's handiwork, to be experienced and recorded for its spiritual power, before man's mortal touch destroyed its purity. The artist came to nature as a pilgrim, and through his heightened sensitivity crystallized and transmitted the wilderness experience to others.

Lane may well have met Emerson personally and almost surely heard him lecture, since he spoke frequently in Boston when Lane was working there. During the 1850's Emerson also appeared in Gloucester almost every year, so Lane must have had some degree of familiarity with his thinking.[2] More to the point, Lane, in his trips down the Maine coast, probably experienced for the first time himself the intense identification with nature of which Emerson spoke. His 1849 *Twilight on the Kennebec,* accordingly, becomes an important expression of the wilderness theme in his own art. That it also represented a new phase in American art may perhaps be best understood by comparing it with earlier paintings of the Maine coast.

American artists of significance had been visiting Maine for several decades. The leaders of the Hudson River School, Thomas Cole and Thomas Doughty, were among the first. Cole was painting on Mount Desert Island in the mid-1830's and again in September, 1844; following the later visit he did his *Frenchman Bay, Mount Desert Island (Ill. 36).* To suggest the dramatic power of the waves dashing against Otter Cliffs he has exaggerated the bulk of these towering rocks by tilting them forward. Like a figure in one of John Martin's Biblical landscapes, Cole's tiny individual atop the cliffs is dwarfed before nature's might, as is the sailboat offshore. Cole pays his debt to the tradition of the Sublime in English painting (especially as seen in the paintings of Martin and Benjamin West), at the same time creating a prototype of the wilderness image in America. Doughty's *Mount Desert Lighthouse (Ill. 37)* takes a similar theme and treats it in an equally personal manner. Desert Rock is a lonely outpost some twenty-five miles offshore, barely visible from the mainland in the best weather. Yet Doughty's Mount Desert Island, behind the rock, appears to be just around the next point of land, and he humanizes the scene with figures and with vessels sailing nearby, adding the comforting touch of smoke from the lighthouse chimney. Both Cole's picture and Doughty's are essentially descriptions of the physical forces of nature. The difference with Lane is that he is principally concerned with revealing nature's spiritual content. Hence, his Maine view almost eliminates the human presence and makes light (with all its symbolism) the dominant element of his landscape.

Doughty's picture was engraved not long after he painted it in 1847, and its wide circulation in this form may well have been a factor in attracting Lane to the Maine coast the following year. Alvan Fisher, another Boston artist, had preceded Lane to the area. From Fisher's visits came one of his best pictures of the Camden Hills (Farnsworth Museum, Rockland, Maine). On August 6, 1848, he made several delicate pencil drawings of Bear Island and Northeast Harbor, Maine, which are strikingly similar to works that Lane would execute a few years later at the same spot. Along with Lane, Benjamin Champney, John F. Kensett, and Frederic E. Church traveled to Mount Desert in the early 1850's, occasionally crossing one another's paths. Church had been Cole's only pupil and doubtless had his teacher's example in mind when he made his own trip, but probably of equal interest and stimulation to Church was Lane's *Twilight on the Kennebec* (*Ill. 35*), which he almost certainly saw at the Art-Union. A New York artist himself, Church had exhibited four pictures there in 1847 and seven more in the same 1849 show with *Twilight*. In his own painting, Church had been slowly working toward expressing similar wilderness images, but to that point his pictures were detailed records of more familiar American scenery in the Hudson River tradition.

There was another aspect of Lane's painting that may have had a catalytic effect on Church and others. Just about this time new oil pigments in the cadmiums became widely available to artists, and Lane seems to have been one of the first to take advantage of them, rendering his glowing effects of light in the new reds, yellows, and oranges.[3] It would appear to be more than coincidental that in 1850 Church made his own decision to go to Maine. In fact, he went to Mount Desert, where Lane was staying, and Lane was aware of his presence in the late summer.[4] Both returned several times during the next few years (see *Ill. 92*), and one can well imagine their paths crossing somewhere. From his first visit alone Church painted several views of Maine that he exhibited later in 1850 at the Art-Union, including three titled *Sunset* or *Twilight*. Two years later he exhibited *Fog off Mount Desert Island* and *Beacon off Mount Desert Island* (Collection Mrs. Vanderbilt Webb, New York), which depicted a fiery red sunset glowing behind the East Bunker Ledge marker at Seal Harbor. Among the dozens of drawings and watercolors that Church made at Mount Desert in the 1850's were a number devoted to capturing the light effects of brilliant Maine sunsets. For example, about 1855 he did the small oil sketch *Bar Harbor* (Olana, Hudson, N.Y.), in which two small sailboats are anchored in the quiet harbor, the dark silhouettes of the mountains visible at the left and the sky filled with sweeping yellows and reds. Church carried over the idea of this wilderness drama, as well as the specific cloud configurations, into his painting *Sunset* of the next year (Munson-Williams-Procter Institute, Utica, N.Y.) and into the apocalyptic *Twilight in the Wilderness* of 1860 (Cleveland Museum of Art).[5]

This latter picture is the culmination of the type, and its display by Church in New York added fresh impetus to the use of hot pigments during the next decade by a number of other American artists—Albert Bierstadt, Sanford Gifford, Martin Johnson Heade, George Inness, and Worthington Whittredge.[6] It would appear, therefore, that Lane's *Kennebec* of 1849 had indeed initiated a new personal and national artistic vision.

The cadmium colors were especially suited to the view of nature's grandeur imagined by Lane and others. In Lane's case, however, his personal friendship with Joseph L. Stevens, Jr., also played a crucial role in bringing the Gloucester artist to Maine. The Stevenses were an old Gloucester family; Joseph, Jr., managed the family's dry goods business there. Interested in cultural and civic affairs, he was active in behalf of the American Art-Union, the Western Art Union, and the local Lyceum movement.[7] In Gloucester he often rowed Lane out into the harbor, as he later did in the small coves of Maine. On one occasion Lane "was hoisted up by some contrivance to the mast-head of a vessel lying in the harbor in order that he might get some particular perspective that he wished to have." [8]

Many years later Stevens wrote a long and illuminating letter to Samuel Mansfield of Gloucester describing his life-long friendship with the painter. It is an important document, for it includes a number of new pieces of information about Lane:

Boston, Oct. 17, 1903

Dear Mr. Mansfield

. . . Lane was much my senior and yet we gradually drifted together. Our earliest approach to friendship was after his abode began in Elm Street as an occupant of the old Prentiss [actually Nymphas Stacy] house, moved then from Pleasant. I was a frequenter of this studio to a considerable extent, yet little compared with my intimacy at the next and last in the new stone house on the hill. Lane's art books and magazines were always at my service and a great inspiration and delight—notably the London Art Journal to which he long subscribed. I have here a little story to tell you. A Castine man came to Gloucester on business that brought the passing of $60 through my hands at 2½% commission. I bought with the $1.50 thus earned Ruskin's Modern Painters, my first purchase of an artbook. I dare say no other copy was then owned in town. If you have not read what that eloquent writer says of clouds, be exhorted to do so.

Lane was frequently in Boston, his sales agent being Balch who was at the head of his guild in those days. So in my Boston visits—I was led to Balch's fairly often —the resort of many artists and the depot of their works. Thus through Lane in various ways I was long in touch with the art world, not only of New England but of New York and Philadelphia. I knew of most picture exhibits and saw many. The coming of the Dusseldorf Gallery to Boston was an event to fix itself in one's memory for all time. What talks of all these things Lane and I had in his studio and by my fireside!

For long series of years I knew nearly every painting he made. I was with him on several trips to the Maine coast where he did much sketching, and sometimes was was [*sic*] his chooser of spots and bearer of materials when he sketched in the home neighborhood. Thus there are many paintings whose growth I saw both from the brush and pencil. For his physical infirmity prevented his becoming an outdoor colorist.

During my two-and-a-half years' absence in the West he kept me so well informed of studio doings that on the resumption of Gloucester home life there were few broken threads to pick up with him. The beginning of my work in Boston some months later changed our relations somewhat without narrowing them.

And so our companionship went on through after years to that sad day when I watched the drawing of his last breath.

Sincerely Yours,
Joseph L. Stevens [9]

Stevens also mentions seeing West's *Death on a Pale Horse* (Philadelphia Museum), a picture of the Sublime that Lane must have seen as well. Of special interest in the letter are the references to Lane's subscription to the *London Art Journal* and his acquaintance with Ruskin's writing, as well as Lane's familiarity with the American "art world." Stevens's own sympathy with these several matters made him a natural companion for the painter, who obviously profited greatly from the exchange of ideas and shared interests, as well as from the practical assistance in traveling to places Lane might sketch or paint. As Stevens notes, he himself went west for awhile. This was in early 1855, when his involvement in the Free Soil issue took him briefly to Kansas for a firsthand investigation into the question of whether slavery should be extended into that state and Nebraska.[10] But he kept in close touch with Lane whenever he was away from Gloucester, and his devotion to the painter lasted until the latter's death, at which time he was executor of Lane's estate. One of his final and most helpful acts was to annotate carefully Lane's many drawings now in Gloucester with remarks about the places and dates of the sketches, the companions on each cruise, and who acquired the paintings subsequently made from the drawings.

Stevens regularly visited his family in Castine, and it was an invitation to stay at the Stevens homestead there that first brought Lane to the Maine coast in 1848.[11] During several subsequent visits he would paint many pictures of the vicinity as well as small oils of the family house and views done especially for presentation to the Stevens family.

Paintings of Maine by Lane from trips in both 1848 and 1849 exist, although some were not actually completed or exhibited until the winter following, and hence in some instances were dated 1849 and 1850, respectively. The summer of 1850 saw the first carefully planned and documented cruise. Reaching Castine by train and boat, Lane and Stevens went out into the countryside nearby, seeking panoramic or scenic vantage points for Lane's sketches. As Stevens had noted, Lane's infirmity made it awkward to carry all the equipment necessary for oil painting out of doors. Thus his drawings are mostly pencil on sketchpad-sized sheets, some joined horizontally for capturing a scene of special breadth. A few have details added in oil or water-color wash; others have shorthand notations by Lane indicating what colors were to be added in the full-scale oils. Lane's reliance on drawing studies further contributed a quality of timelessness to the later paintings, because they permitted him to distill his memory of a place as he painted his oils later in the studio.

Castine is situated on a hillside at the end of a narrow peninsula extending into the northern part of Penobscot Bay. The Stevens house was some distance up from the waterfront and afforded a fine view of the marine activity there and in the bay beyond. Nearby were Fort George and Fort Treble, reminders of the town's involvement in the wars of the nation's early years, but it was the extensive vistas from the rising fields and hilly outcroppings that appealed most to Lane's eye. Typical are two paintings he did of Castine from above the town (*Ill. 38* and Witherle Memorial Library, Castine). The high vantage point is reminiscent of some of Lane's earlier lithographs (see *Ills. 5, 8,* and *16*) but is even closer to the Baltimore view of the same year (*Ills. 17* and *18*), where the figures stand in a field curving diagonally across the immediate foreground. In the company of both Stevenses, Lane did a similar drawing, *Castine from Wasson's Hill, Brooksville, Maine* (private collection).

Later, in August of 1850, Lane and Stevens chartered the boat *General Gates,* with Captain Getchell in charge, and the cruise inspired a small oil of the boat under way across the Penobscot (private collection). The goal of the cruise was Mount Desert Island to the east, whose sloping mountains and picturesque coves had already attracted Cole, Doughty, and others. Their pictures and various descriptions of the area were known to the Castine party. Stevens described their voyage in a long and fascinating article that he subsequently wrote for the *Gloucester Telegraph:*

This supposed barren and desolate place can boast of scenery so grand and beautiful as to be unsurpassed by any on the whole American coast. We had understood so much from hearsay of the remarkable and picturesque range of mountains on the island, the fine harbors, and beautiful sound, that even abating liberally for enthusiastic exaggeration, we were certain of being amply repaid for a sail of fifty miles each way. . . .

Baffling winds and calms, the first day compelled a stoppage for the night half way at Naskeag. Here our tent was pitched, a convenient haycock borrowed for the purpose of making the ground a little more comfortable than it otherwise might be and "them Injuns" as some of the lookers-on supposed them, thus enjoyed a comfortable rest. The next morning we received an early visit from the lord of the Manor, a loquacious and well-disposed gentleman who prefaced his sociability by supposing the newcomers were on a "fishing discussion."

It is a grand sight approaching Mount Desert from the westward, to behold the mountains gradually open upon the view. At first there seems to be only one upon the island. Then one after another they unfold themselves until at last some ten or twelve stand up there in grim outline. Sailing abreast the range, the beholder finds them assuming an infinite diversity of shapes, and it sometimes requires no great stretch of imagination to fancy them hugh mammoth and mastodon wading out from the main. With such a beautiful prospect to wonder at and admire, now wafted along by light winds, then entirely becalmed for a time, we were slowly carried into Southwest Harbor. Here, from what seems to be a cave on the mountain side, is Somes Sound, reaching up through a great gorge seven miles into the heart of the island. It varies much in width, the extremes being perhaps a half mile and two miles, is of great depth, and contains no hindrance to free navigation. An intervening point concealed the entrance until we had nearly approached it [*Plate V*], and the sails passing in before us disappeared as if by enchantment.

It was toward the close of as lovely an afternoon as summer can bestow that we entered this beautiful inlet. Much had been anticipated, the reality exceeded all expectations. There were none of those gusts which are said to dart suddenly down from the treacherous mountains to the dismay of unwary boatmen, but with breezes seldom strong enough to ripple the quiet water, the old boat went leisurely up the current, and so engrossed had we become in the grandness of the scenery on every hand, and so illusive the distances were that it seemed as if we could be but halfway up the inlet when we passed through the narrows into the basin forming the head of the Sound [*Ill. 39*]. Just as the sun was setting we encamped opposite the settlement, at the entrance of the miniature bay, on an island well wooded and covered with a profusion of berries. . . .

An attempt was made next day to ascend the highest and boldest of the mountains that skirt the Sound. But after a long and laborious scramble up among the rocks and fallen trees we had reached a peak but half way to the summit and stopped to rest there, when a thunder-storm burst with savage fury. We seemed to be in the very midst of the cloud and tempest. Advance we could not, neither could one recede in such darkness and blinding rain. Here then, in the bleak surface of the mountain, with no shelter but a jagged rock against which we could crouch when the wind blew strongly from the opposite quarter, we were forced to receive the drenching of a pitiless storm. Yet it was a scene of such sublimity up there where the lightnings seemed playing in their favorite haunts and the thunders reverberated in prolonged and deafening peals, among the trembling hills, that we were not unwilling occupants of this novel situation. . . .

It is a misnomer to call such an island Mount Desert. Some of the grand old mountains which have been burned over showing nothing but the large ledges of sienite and charred pine trees, with here and there a little shrubbery struggling for life look dreary and desolate, but they stand among the others covered with a luxuriant growth. Our pilot told us of a Frenchman who once got lost here for some weeks, when his country held this region, and so gave the title to it. But it seems the island has begun to get its dues—one of its three townships is now called Eden. The beauties of this place is well known and appreciated among artists. We heard of Bonfield and Williams who had reluctantly left but a short time before. Fisher had spent several weeks there. Champney and Kensett were then in another part of the island and we have reason to believe that Church and some others were in the immediate vicinity. Lane who was with us, made good additions to his portfolio. But how unsatisfying a few days to an artist, when many months sketching would scarcely suffice amid such exhaustless wealth of scenery.[12]

Halfway up Somes Sound, Lane made a sketch looking back toward the entrance; it bears the following inscription by Stevens at the bottom: "Lane made this sketch in the stern of the General Gates as we slowly sailed up the Sound of Mt. Desert on a lovely afternoon of our first excursion there. He painted a small picture from this, his first sketch of that scenery. It was sold by Balch to Mrs. Josiah Quincy, Jr." [13]

Of their anchorage off Bar Island at the head of the Sound, Lane made at least one drawing, which served as the basis for a later oil, *Bar Island and Mount Desert Mountains from the Bay in Front of Somes Settlement* (Ill. 39). The drawing is remarkably complete, lacking only the figures and vessels in the foreground (and, of course, the color). Lane added two other personal touches to the finished oil: The bright red longjohns drying on the forestay at the right and the little rowboat at the center, with Stevens and himself rowing ashore. The painting also reveals how carefully he designed his compositions. Consider, for example, the way he has played off the three major vessels in the foreground against the three pieces of land behind and the three slopes of mountains in the distance. It is a design, of course, that appears to be utterly natural and realistic, yet it possesses a coherence of organization and harmony of detail that denote the artist's controlling presence. Lane's other drawings in the area included *"General Gates" at anchor off Our Encampment at Bar Island in Somes Sound, Mount Desert, Maine; North East Harbor, Mount Desert* ("taken from the boat 'General Gates' at anchor"); and *Mount Desert Mountains, from Bar Island, Somes Sound* ("Picture painted from this sketch once in my [Stevens's] possession and afterward sold by W. Y. Balch").

The most vivid way of illustrating the meaning of the Maine experience for Lane's work is to compare two of his paintings a decade apart, the first from an early trip, the second from one of his last and very best years of painting. Both are views of *Owl's Head* at the southern end of Penobscot Bay (*Ills. 40* and *41*). Just as the prominent slopes of Mount Desert appealed to Lane, so too he became fascinated with the distinctive double humps of Owl's Head, in that day not yet covered with firs. The earlier painting, dating from 1852, is essentially a narrative picture, in the manner of his Gloucester pictures of the 1840's; that is, he is primarily concerned with the description of physical forms and activities, from the exaggerated contours of the headland itself to the various vessels prominently sailing by. In the foreground, the red-shirted figure in the small sailboat catches our attention, as if inviting the spectator to join the fun. In a manner typical of his early style Lane paints the waves with strong color and relatively thick applications of pigment (see *Ill.* 22). In other words, the technique of painting itself reinforces a sense of action with almost literary overtones. (After 1850 Lane used this style only intermittently [*Ill. 91*].) Subtle and distinctive as the handling of light is—in falling across the two slopes of Owl's Head and catching the upper sails on the boats to the right—its role is still a marginal one, subordinate to the almost tactile sense of action.

In the 1862 version, instead of the close-up view, with its invitation to participate actively in the scene, we are now given a more distant and detached vantage point. We no longer focus on the action in the foreground, closed in by the near horizon made by the headland; we are removed spectators from the quiet of the beach, uninvolved in the turbulent tossing implied by the earlier work. Even the time of day is less connotative of human activity: The broad afternoon, with its fair-weather breeze for sailing, has become a transitory moment before sunrise. We are drawn to look beyond the single, contemplative figure, unidentified in any way (for we see him from the back only), deep into space—into the sky, into the light. Lane has set up a psychic as well as a physical distance, and with it, a whole new mood. His changed vision is now complete.

For light has become the foremost element; its gentle promise belongs to nature's more intangible spirit. Lane's whole later view is suffused with pale tonalities: a translucent pink on the sails and the lighthouse from the sun's first rays, thin yellows on the water's surface, cool blues for the distant hills, and soft greens for the near landscape and reflections in the water. Lane now applies his pigments with a new thinness: In some places the weave of the underlying canvas is visible (making the cleaning of the later works especially difficult); replacing his previous uses of impasto are very thin glazes, more suited to the lucidity of this later painting of light.

Most revealing of all, however, are Lane's compositional distortions. In the first version the exaggeration of the headland's contours is perhaps overly obvious, although in keeping with a concentration on factuality and physicality. In the 1862 painting Lane makes a less overt but far more arbitrary change in the geography. As comparison with a photograph (*Ill. 42*) of the spot indicates, he has shifted the location of the distant Camden Hills from their actual location to the right of Owl's Head to the left side. His reason is purely aesthetic: to balance, slightly off center, the two hillsides on either side of the boat's vertical axis. This fact is important to recognize in Lane's later style, because it is a fundamental clue to the achievement of his mature art. Such a basic artistic decision once again reflects how much this painter, commonly thought to be merely a careful realist, has gone beyond the realism of the external world to reveal as well something of nature's internal order and harmony. This latter concern is a primary element in luminism, of which Lane was one of the earliest exponents with his paintings beginning in the 1850's. The notion that the inner or higher values of nature might be expressed through color and pure light explains why so many of Lane's later landscapes are literally given over to clouds or sky. This is why *Twilight on the Kennebec* (*Ill. 35*) portends so much both for Lane's art and for that of many of his contemporaries at mid-century.

CHAPTER SIX
REPRESENTATION OF SCENERY
OFTEN ADMIRED

Lane returned with Stevens to Castine in 1851, the year in which he discovered Owl's Head. One charming small oil, now in poor condition, was painted at the Stevens house: *Penobscot Bay from the Southwest Chamber Window* (William A. Farnsworth Library and Art Museum, Rockland, Maine). Three drawings done on this visit, one of the *Camden Mountains* and the other two of *Owl's Head,* were "taken from the steamer's deck in passing." The younger Stevens was the first owner of a small oil of the Camden scene but later sold it through Balch, a Boston dealer. The drawing *Northeast View of Owl's Head* (*Ill. 43*), dated August, 1851, has a more interesting history. Stevens had noted on it, "This sketch was painted in moonlight effect and presented to my mother." Returning from his trip that summer, Lane set to work directly on the painting. He completed it within a month and presented it as a gift of thanks to his hosts. Both Mr. and Mrs. Stevens wrote letters of gratitude, with Joseph Stevens responding as follows:

Castine, January 29, 1851

My dear Sir,

. . . I can no longer defer the expressions of our warmest acknowledgements for a present, in itself so valuable, and endeared to us by many associations, as a representation of scenery often admired, and which I have many times wished could be transferred to canvas, although very far from that wish would ever be gratified [*sic*]. You must permit me, however, to say that the Painting, valuable as it is as a work of Art, and pleased as I may be as the possessor of it, is less appreciated by us than the delicate and very generous manner in which its acceptance has been tendered. . . . I feel, too, under great obligations for the Drawing of the "Siege"—I had no expectations you could have produced anything so good from so rough a copy. I shall have it framed for preservation and future reference. Several gentlemen who have called in to see the painting have expressed a desire to have a drawing from you of our town, similar to yours of Gloucester, which they much admire, and, if lithographed, I have no doubt copies enough could be disposed of to remunerate you. . . . There are several points of view, which you did not see, and to which it will be my pleasure, next summer, to carry you. I know many of our citizens would be gratified to have this done by you. Our house we shall expect to be your home, and if as you suggested in Gloucester, you should come in your Boat, this place could be made the rendezvous, from whence you could start to any place that convenience and inclination might dictate. I will only say that my wife and myself will spare no efforts on our part to make your visit agreeable, and perhaps useful. You have not or did not exhaust all the beauties of Mt. Desert scenery, and perhaps there may be other spots in our Bay, that you may think worthy of the pencil. . . .

We look forward with great pleasure, to your visit next summer, providence permitting, and in the meantime beg leave to assure you of the sincere esteem and respect.

of yours, most truly
Joseph L. Stevens [1]

The location of the painting is no longer known, though a glance at two of Lane's many pictures of Owl's Head (*Ills. 40* and *43*) show how intrigued he was with recording its changing aspect from different points of view. In addition, an examination of his various preliminary studies alongside the finished oils gives further information about his methods of working, which he seems to have refined with his first voyages to Maine. The *Owl's Head* drawing of 1851 is typical of the several dozen drawings now in the collection of the Cape Ann Historical Association. Most of them average ten to twelve inches high, though some with sheets pasted together frequently measure thirty to forty inches in width. Together, they exhibit a wide range of drafting techniques, from the brief, impressionistic strokes used primarily to define trees or shrubbery and the long, uninterrupted lines for indicating contours of large shapes or shorelines, to broad strokes and shading for volumes and surfaces. Almost never is there any indication of sources of light and shadows (see also *Ill. 65*); the drawings are largely of major outlines and contours. A much smaller number of sketches have additional touches of watercolor or oil wash to emphasize further volumes (*Ill. 53*) or to recall detailed effects of color. An example of the latter is his watercolor *Castine Harbor and Town* of 1851 (*Ill. 44*), the preliminary study for an oil painting now in Witherle Memorial Library in Castine. Attaching two sketch sheets together, Lane made his panoramic view in pencil and then filled in the foreground with a green watercolor wash, drew in the vessel, and, finally, used touches of pink and green for some of the houses and landscape of the town. His final notations consisted of marking on a number of the buildings the letters *R, Y,* and *B,* standing for the colors to be used in the subsequent painting.

A few of the drawings are more finished. Such is the case with his *Study of Ships* (*Ill. 45*), in which the careful pyramidal grouping of the vessels, the instinctively arranged pattern of light and dark sails, the sense of air, and the intimation of light falling on the hulls and the water indicate that Lane himself may have considered this a finished piece of work, a suspicion reinforced by our knowledge that the drawing was a gift to Stevens. That Lane felt it a more personal achievement than usual is clear from the signature, one of the few cases in which he signed in his own script rather than in the formal printed letters he customarily used for his drawings and paintings. Still, the drawing may well have been originally intended as a study, as it can be directly related to the groupings of ships that Lane often included in his large views of New York and Boston harbors during the 1850's (*Plate III; Ill. 76*). Similarly, the small oil sketch *Study of Vessels* (*Ill. 46*), although highly accomplished, is but one more variation on the pencil drawing. One senses that here Lane was taking initial steps to define pictorial space and the tangibility of volumes existing in that space. Now the sails hang with their own weight, and the hulls are modeled fully. A more cursory type of study in his drawing *A Topsail* (*Ill. 47*), at once more intimate, yet monumental, in its simple strength.

Lane rarely made oil sketches. Along with the *Study of Vessels,* his study *Plant and Two Figures* and *Seashore Sketch* (*Ills. 48* and *49*) are notable. He used oil, pen, and pencil on canvas for *Plant and Men,* signing his name to each image. The *Seashore Sketch* is the only known study so free and impressionistic in its execution. Here he was experimenting with capturing the effects of rough seas and turbulent skies; he has done so with the strokes of paint applied thickly and vigorously. This manner appears less frequently, though regularly, in the paintings of his later career (*see Ills. 59* and *91*). Equally rare is Lane's use of photographs in his preliminary work, as seen in *Steamer "Harvest Moon" Lying at Wharf in Portland* (*Ill. 50*). The photograph, however, played an important, if occasional, role in Lane's construction of his later paintings. Stevens has noted: "Painting made by Lane for Lang & Delano, India Wharf, Boston, from this photograph," and "introducing her into a sketch of Portland Harbor taken on our visit in August 1863." Lane methodically ruled off the photograph into quadrants for transposition to another pencil drawing, *Looking up Portland Harbor,* which bears the remark: "Sketch made for a picture for J. H. B. Lang in which to introduce steamer Harvest Moon." In fact, Lane ruled off into larger quadrants a number of his later drawings (*Ill. 51*), illustrating his concern with accuracy and for consistency in the changes of scale from photograph to drawing to painting. Both Gene McCormick and Barbara Novak have discussed the role of such measurement in Lane's desire for precision in his art.[2] Not only were the clarity and realism of photography particularly suited to his views of nature, but the process of division and measurement involved were fundamental devices for enabling him to define and record the dimensions of physical reality. This process was closely related to his careful ordering of elements in his oil paintings. In other words, every composition underwent a refinement of order and balance, of distribution and spacing. Thus, in a curious way, the outer eye of the camera actually assisted Lane in clarifying what was physically unseen—what is called by some the moral order of nature. For him, as for Emerson, the physical and metaphysical worlds were inextricably related.

Looking at Lane's pencil sketch *Westward View from near East End of Railroad Bridge* and an oil painting based on it (*Ills. 51* and *52*), one can see that the principal outlines of the scene are all present in the study. He has, however, ruled off the drawing vertically in two places and drawn a new base line higher up from the bottom of the page, thus strengthening the sense of breadth, and this change is carried over to the painting. Lane made three oils from the drawing, but the one shown here is the only one whose present location is known. (The picturesque spot that Lane portrays is often referred to as "Done Fudging," because people bring their boats ashore at this point after muddling about in the tidal marshes of the river.)

Between the drawing *Gloucester from the Outer Harbor* and the painted version (*Ills. 53* and *54*), both done in 1852, Lane made few changes in the details and scale of his shoreline, but he markedly shifted his vantage point. The drawing is one of the few with watercolor additions, here presumably to help contrast the Old Fort at the right with the rest of the town waterfront. The oil is one of Lane's strongest works, possessing an intensity of light reminiscent of his first major oil of Gloucester in 1844 (*Plate I*). As in the later lithographs, there is now that great economy of design, as well as the careful play of light and dark tonalities, and, as far as subject matter is concerned, the delicate equilibrium between physical activities and the intangible mood introduced by light and atmosphere.

When the painting was donated to the town of Gloucester in 1913, the

Telegraph carried a detailed description of it.[3] Lane had painted the work
for Sidney Mason, the Gloucester businessman who had moved to New York
some years before and who in 1850 had commissioned the views of New
York and San Juan harbors. His descendants presented the work to Gloucester as a memento of Mason's long-time affection for the place.

A pair of Gloucester views done a few years later shows a different aspect
of the town: its rural charm and peacefulness. They also reveal Lane's fascination with depicting the same spot from a slightly different vantage point—
reinterpreting the same scene, so to speak, at another moment in time.
Gloucester from Brookbank (*Ill. 55*) is probably the view recorded on November 8 in Samuel Sawyer's 1856 Account Book as "Lane—Homestead—
$100."[4] The other painting, *The Sawyer Homestead* (Sawyer Free Library,
Gloucester), represented here by its preliminary drawing (*Ill. 56*), is almost
certainly the one Sawyer mentioned in his Diary on August 25, 1864: "Called
to see Mr. Lane to make a sketch of old Homestead for Houghtons—gone to
Boston."[5] Sawyer was one of Gloucester's most prominent citizens; he had
traveled widely but was also active locally, playing a prominent role in establishing the local Lyceum, the library, and Ravenswood Park at the western
edge of town. He encouraged Lane and other artists, and his collection included their works as well as those by Europeans. The two views of his estate
illustrated here show the field in front of his house, bordered by the sloping
fence, with a glimpse out to Gloucester's outer harbor beyond. The painting
from the mid-1850's is lush with the greens of summer, and on the whole it
is a picture in Lane's earlier manner: There is a great deal of visual information to catch the eye, from the cows and great foreground rocks to the sailboats scattered near and far on the water beyond, with men raising or lower-
ing sails. A broad, full sunlight suffuses the scene with a sense of optimism
and contentment. While the painting of the 1860's that resulted from the
Sawyer Homestead drawing retains the dark greens in the landscape, Lane
now chooses to show it in late afternoon, with the sky a deeper blue above
and the pink light of the setting sun just catching the top of the house and
the sails of the boat in the harbor. More significant is the de-emphasis on
those narrative details of the earlier work. Instead of the cows, outbuildings,
and boats, all competing for attention, the complex of buildings is absorbed
almost as a single unit into the surrounding trees, and only one vessel is seen
on the water. Two other small drawings are worth noting here, because, although undated, they possibly belong to Lane's two views of the Sawyer
place. One appears to be of the large foreground rock (*Ill. 57*) in *Gloucester*

from Brookbank, and the other, of a tree (*Ill. 58*), could well be any of those nearby. Even in such unpretentious works one finds Lane's remarkable ability to create images of both delicacy and strength.

In another pair of pictures, both done in 1852, Lane shows two sequential moments in time. In the first (Collection George Lewis, Boston), a three-master sails precariously close to the lee shore of Stage Fort Rocks on her way out of Gloucester harbor in heavy seas. Choosing the same vantage point for the second painting, Lane shows the vessel wrecked on the rocks (*Ill. 59*). Two of her masts have broken off and are in the water, while the crew is assisting with the rescue of the passengers in a lifeboat. Some have already reached the rocks; the beret and tartan knickers on one figure would suggest that the vessel was making an ocean-going passage. But Lane arouses our interest without being explicit: The name board of the vessel has been partially broken off, leaving only the letters "WIL." Among his stormy paintings in the dramatic Dutch manner, this is one of the best resolved.

From reviewing these various approaches to his painting, it becomes apparent that Lane had evolved methodical and thorough habits of work by the early 1850's. His first trips to Maine increased the necessity of working from initial pencil drawings, and these he developed into a finished form of their own, while leaving the matter of color and light to the oils done in the studio. In 1852 he and Stevens planned an even more elaborate cruise around the Penobscot Bay and Mount Desert areas, primarily to visit scenic places that Lane might sketch. A notation on a drawing of *Duck Harbor* listed the group as "F. H. Lane, artist/ W. H. Tilden, J. L. Stevens, jr., G. F. Tilden, S. Adams, jr. Companions / Sloop Superior, Getchel, Pilot from Castine," and another 1852 drawing indicates that William H. Witherle, also from Castine, was with the group. This time, after sailing down Eggemoggin Reach, they headed south to Isle au Haut, which afforded Lane a new vista of the islands at the southern end of Blue Hill Bay. The *Superior* anchored in Duck Harbor; then, leaving Isle au Haut, it sailed east to Mount Desert Rock, some twenty-five miles off shore in the Gulf of Maine, where Lane made the drawing *North Westerly View of Mount Desert Rock* ("Aug. 1852, Taken from deck of Sloop Superior at anchor").

From the rock the group sailed north toward Mount Desert, pausing at Southwest Harbor and the southern end of Somes Sound, and here Lane made two more sketches, one of which resulted in the beautiful oil *Entrance of Somes Sound from Southwest Harbor* (*Plate V*), thought by some to be his best work. Looking north to the entrance of the Sound, he has caught the scene in the steely glare of the Maine light in summer. The pale blue tonalities of the whole picture are punctuated by white sails on an anchored vessel, occasional patches of dark green pines, and a few houses on the far shore. The still calm that often comes at midday is conveyed by the sharp clarity of the reflections on the water's mirror surface. The view, seen first on his 1850 trip, must have had a lasting impact on Lane's memory; he returned to the same place yet again in 1855, when he did a drawing (*Ill. 65*) close in composition to the 1852 oil. Here, especially, he must have felt a pristine tranquility that seemed to embody nature's transcendent beauty. Seeking those havens wherein the spirit of man might be coextensive with the spirit of the natural world, Lane identified Southwest Harbor as such a place. Once more there were subtle compositional and topographical adjustments for aesthetic reasons: In this instance he slightly altered the sloping contours of the mountains in the distance, so that their shape might complement, in particular, the foreground rocks. Essentially the painting emphasizes the restful horizontals of both the foreground and the far shoreline, while offering subtle counterpoints in the masts of the vessel, which cut above the horizon, and in the reflection of her sails crossing the water to the front. In addition, the touch of red in the man's shirt in the left foreground is picked up by another figure in the right background. Thus all parts of the composition are harmoniously linked together. In every respect the painting represents Lane at his most poetic and evocative.

If Maine was the source of some of Lane's best work in 1852, he was also active on his return to Gloucester and Boston. He completed a hazy early morning view of Pigeon Cove on Cape Ann, called *Sunrise Through Mist: Pigeon Cove, Gloucester* (Shelburne Museum, Shelburne, Vt.). Intermittent work on ship portraits continued. For example, the small watercolor *Brig "Agenosa" in Gloucester Harbor,* the drawing *Tow Boat,* and *The Ship "Mermaid"* (Collection David L. May, Acton, Mass.) all date from that period. Of more significance are two works of the area very different in subject and handling but equally monumental in effect. *Ships in Ice off Ten Pound Island* (*Ill. 60*) suggests extraordinary spaciousness, but its actual size is relatively small. It is Lane's only known winter scene, and his characteristic treatment of cool atmospheric effects serves the subject well. He appears to limit his palette to a near monochromy of whites and grays, appropriate to the icebound scene, but the eye soon discovers a wide range of pale colors—soft greens and blues in the sky and ice and tans and browns in the boats and sails. The small size of the figures and the low, almost uninterrupted horizon add to the feeling of expansive depth. Carefully placing the central vessels off center, Lane groups around them the two other schooners, the pole in the ice, and the empty row boat, with each occupying a corner of the composition.

In contrast to the size of this work stands one of his largest pictures, *Half Way Rock* (*Ill. 61*), so called because of the marker's location between Gloucester and Marblehead. Again it is largely a design of juxtapositions: between the sails in sunlight and shadow; the strong horizon line and the masts crossing it; the rock as the center of attention and its actual placement to the left of center; the repeated patterns respectively of clouds and waves; the vessels balanced on either side of the rock; and lastly the colors—a red-shirted figure against the dark green water and the pale yellow clouds in complement to a blue sky. As in all Lane's mature works, such details as sails and figures are fully convincing; that is, they are drawn and painted with a complete understanding of their functions and range of actions. Of its type— paint applied vigorously and thickly, a scene of action rather than of contemplation—*Half Way Rock* is an unsurpassed example. Lane has put into it only what is necessary, and that restraint imbues both man and his vessels with a feeling of the heroic. The choice of this isolated rock recalls his drawing *Mount Desert Rock* (1852). The offshore view was becoming increasingly characteristic of Lane: It was often a quieter and more reflective vantage point than most landbound, and therefore populated, spots.

Not surprisingly, Lane returned to Half Way Rock to paint it in moonlight (*Ill. 62*). In this version he chooses a closer point of view and juxtaposes only one group of vessels to the rock—both solutions more appropriate to the greater intimacy of the picture. Lane did few moonlight scenes. Here again, he may have been inspired by Washington Allston, whose *Moonlit Landscape* of 1819 (Museum of Fine Arts, Boston) he could well have seen in Boston in the 1830's or 1840's. Allston's pictures were frequently on exhibit there in those years, and Lane's colleague Champney talks expressly of seeing the older painter's "many classic landscapes."[6] There would appear to be much of Allston in this work: Its combination of memory and observation, a classical quality of balance and restraint—to which Champney alludes—and, particularly, the compositional device of the central axis of moonlight as the real focus of the picture. The rendering of moonlight was for Lane an extension of his fascination with those hours of dawn and dusk that so preoccupied him in Maine. Of equal or greater expressive significance than the undeniable Romanticism inherent in the physical setting is the dreamlike quality of brooding unreality exuded by this shadowy half-light. One can almost imagine the artist, even as he is looking more carefully than ever at the exterior world, turning inward to view the dark recesses of an inner vision. Whatever the explanation, Lane produced some moonlight views in the closing years of his life, which may well be a metaphorical recognition of his own mortality.

CHAPTER SEVEN
BEAUTIFUL PICTURES
WITH PLEASING ASSOCIATIONS

Lane continued to submit works to the major annual exhibitions in New York and Boston during the 1850's. For example, at the Art-Union in 1852 was *Marine View* ("a sunset scene. On the left are a promontory and lighthouse, and on the right a ship lying at anchor."), which A. Edwards bought for fifty dollars in a sale held December 15 to 17. Besides the major galleries in Boston and New York, a number of others invited Lane's work. His paintings were on view at the Massachusetts Charitable Mechanics Association as early as 1841 and 1844; the Albany Gallery of Fine Arts made him a member in 1848 and showed paintings by him two years later.

During the winter of 1853, Mrs. Joseph Stevens again wrote Lane to thank him for a picture given to the family:

Castine, February 9th, 1853

Dear Sir:

We received a few days since, the painting of our daughter's residence, executed by you. It affords us a twofold gratification, in being able to recognize in it, the home of a dear child, and of knowing that you still remember us. Please to accept in return our sincere and heartfelt thanks. It is indeed a beautiful picture, independent of the pleasing associations connected with it. . . .

[My husband] says the "General Gates" is destroyed, yet he thinks Mr. Getchell will have a better boat, but he hopes, as has been suggested, that you will be able to come down in your own yacht.

Again, allow me to express our sincere thanks for the little "Brown Cottage."

Yours very respectfully,
D. L. Stevens [1]

Although there are no drawings specifically dated 1853 or 1854, Lane did a painting of a Maine lighthouse at twilight (Collection H. J. Heinz, III,

Pittsburgh, Pa.) in 1854. That he made his usual visits to Maine in those summers is suggested by a letter to the Boston *Courier* in 1855, who noted that "Mr. F. H. Lane of Gloucester . . . visits here nearly every summer."[2] Certainly belonging to this period in style are his several views of the Camden Hills, with sailing vessels sitting idly off the entrance to Camden Harbor, their sails hanging in the still air and late afternoon light (private collection and *Ill. 63*). These pictures vary little among themselves compositionally: The profile of the hills is always the same, and only the placement of the vessels in the foreground is altered. In such cases Lane usually copied one picture from another, making minor variations, when he had an additional commission or wanted to make a gift of the same view. Of interest here are the large lumber schooners in the foreground, so typical of that day. Penobscot Bay was often dotted with these vessels, heavily laden with either wood or granite, in passage from eastern Maine to Portland or Boston. Sometimes Lane would show them under way in rough waters (Sawyer Free Library, Gloucester, and *Ill. 91*).

Gloucester continued to provide subjects for his pencil and brush. Dating from the mid-1850's is *Fresh Water Cove from Dolliver's Neck* (Museum of Fine Arts, Boston), so named from Champlain's landing at that site in 1607 in search of fresh water. During the summer of 1852 he completed *Salem Harbor (Plate VI)*, one of a series of harbor views done in Gloucester and especially in Boston during the mid-1850's. A brilliant blue sky fills much of the canvas, counterpointed only by the white of the sails and now familiar red-shirted figure in the foreground dory. Particularly striking are the alternating light and dark sails on the three-master to the left and the down-to-earth touch of the patches on the sails in the foreground. Just above the patches are Lane's initials.

The next year Lane finished *Boston Harbor (Ill. 64)*; the time is now late afternoon rather than midday. The open view into the far distance to the state-house dome contrasts with the closed composition of *Yacht "Northern Light" in Boston Harbor (Ill. 23)* of a decade earlier. Another Boston Harbor view (Collection Robert Bacon, Woods Hole, Mass.) of 1852 is similarly composed. A third view in this group, done in 1854, (The White House, Washington) describes another combination of shipping activities, the details of Boston's shoreline, and the clouds lit by the setting sun. These views of Gloucester and Boston could only have been done after Lane's visits to the Maine coast and the consequent changes in his style that occurred around 1850.

While such pictures held the strongest interest for Lane for much of the rest of his career, he periodically shifted over to working with heavier appli-

cations of paint and to treating subjects full of action and drama. He seems to
have worked in both styles at the same time, and typical of his more dramatic
approach were a group of pictures showing vessels in rough seas, most of them
dating from the mid-1850's such as *Three Master in Rough Seas, A Smart
Blow,* and *A Rough Sea* (all in Cape Ann Historical Association). This rather
Dutch style was one that Lane tried early in his career, for example, in *Cunard Liner "Britannia"* (*Ill.* 22); and one he returned to in his last years, notably in *Lumber Schooner in a Storm* (*Ill.* 91).[3] In fact, the last painting on his
easel at the time of his death was the oil *Two Ships in Rough Waters.* Regarding one of these paintings, Helen Mansfield described her brother's negotiations with the artist:

> My brother, James H. Mansfield, had one of the most beautiful Lane's I have ever
> seen—a picture of a barque dismasted, and rolling in a heavy sea. The touch was
> very soft and beautiful. Jerome Elwell said: "That sky was painted con amore."
>
> It was bought under peculiar conditions. Mr. Lane was not willing to sell it
> outright, because he said the man who ordered it might call for it—so my brother
> held it conditionally, he was to give it up if the man ever appeared, but he never
> did. It was a sailor, who had been in a wreck of the kind, and described it to
> Mr. Lane.[4]

In the late summer of 1855 Lane planned another extensive cruise from
Castine with Stevens.[5] With Joseph S. Hooper of Gloucester, who was soon to
move to Dubuque, Iowa, Lane traveled to Rockland in September, where
they met Stevens. This year their cruise was to be in two parts, the first around
the Rockland and Camden area of the Penobscot. They chartered a boat and
set off to sail around Owl's Head, where Lane wanted to make several drawings. The earliest is annotated, "First sketch on our cruise. Taken from our
boat in the early forenoon of a beautiful day, lying north of Owl's Head—
on our approach from Rockland." He then made at least three other sketches
of the headland from slightly different vantage points. The two prominent
slopes constantly changed in their relationship to each other, at the same time
presenting a powerful image of natural topography. Possibly the party spent
the night at Linwood Cottage in Rockport, where a photograph of the "Residence of L. Emery [was] Presented by him to F. H. Lane." Next they sailed
north toward Camden, so that Lane might make similar sketches of the hills
rising behind the town. His first drawing here was a "Sketch taken on the
second day of our cruise while going from Rockland to Camden." A second
drawing was of the *Camden Mountains,* and from it Lane later painted an oil
for Stevens "as a generous souvenir of our excursion." The last sketch of the

day was *Camden Mountains and Harbor from North of Negro Island,* executed "toward sundown of our second day's cruise. The picture painted from this sketch [*Ill. 63*] was sold by W. Y. Balch to a gentleman of Maine." They spent their second night in Camden Harbor and the next morning started back. Lane made one last drawing of the *Camden Mountains,* "taken from the boat on our return to Rockland."

The second part of the group's trip was another cruise to Mount Desert; they apparently headed directly for Southwest Harbor, which Lane had drawn in both 1850 and 1852. His sketch *Entrance of Somes Sound from Back of the Island House at Southwest Harbor, Mount Desert* (*Ill. 65*) is among his most varied in execution. His use of shading for Brown Mountain in the right distance and some of the trees in the foreground hints of more volume and texture than he was accustomed to including. He appears to be concerned with rendering contours, experimenting with different kinds of pencil strokes and degrees of definition, as the outlines of the mountain slopes indicate. Using the more horizontal format of three sheets pasted together, he also drew *Looking Westerly from Eastern Side of Somes Sound near the Entrance* (*Ill. 66*), in which, rather than contours, he accents the geological structure of the rock formations. Most of his time on this part of the trip was devoted to Bear Island off the entrance to Northeast Harbor. As was his habit, he now drew Bear Island from a number of vantage points (*Ill. 67*), and from several of the sketches paintings resulted (*Ill. 68*). A painting of *Bear Island* was "presented to Joseph S. Hooper of Dubuque, Iowa, as a memento of our excursions." An oil view from the Southeast shows the island at dawn, with pinks and reds bringing the scene out of the darkness of night. In many ways it is a picture of creation—the meaning and promise of dawn, seen at its purest in this isolated fragment of nature.

As another tribute to his friendship with Stevens, Lane began work in September, 1855, on his lithograph *Castine from Hospital Island* (*Ill. 21*), which Stevens published. Either just before or following his journey to Mount Desert, he made a panoramic sketch of Castine, using six sheets of paper pasted together to record every aspect of the town's shoreline. Also from this trip, Lane submitted to the Boston Athenaeum an oil titled *Mount Desert Light House* (1855).

The appeal of that mountainous island called him back the following summer, when he again worked on several paintings of the island and of Blue Hill to the west. One was *Off Mount Desert Island, Maine* (*Ill. 69*), which carefully juxtaposes the sailing vessels against the silhouettes of the mountains behind. Lane adjusts the formations of the clouds to echo the curves of the same slopes. In 1856 he also completed *Off Mount Desert Island* (Brooklyn Museum), a sunset view, and *Sunrise on the Maine Coast* (*Ill. 70*), with Mount Desert in the background. Anchored offshore is Lane's sailboat, and in the right foreground, seated on a rock, is the artist himself sketching in the first rays of dawn. Over and over again the tranquil and transitory nature of dawn embodied for him the serene spiritual identification man might make with nature. As such, paintings in this manner stand as quintessential statements of the luminist movement. The same was true of the radiant light in *Blue Hill, Maine* (*Plate VII*), which, although based on a pencil drawing of August, 1851 (private collection), was probably not painted until the mid-1850's. The view is taken from Parker Point looking back westward to the town and the hill behind. As in his pictures of Owl's Head and Somes Sound, Lane made subtle changes in the actual contour of Blue Hill for artistic reasons—the peak is slightly more acute and thus more imposing. As in Cézanne's late views of Mont Sainte-Victoire, the visual distortion gives a truer image of the mountain's nature than any photographically accurate rendering of the topography could.

Increasingly during the later 1850's, Lane was applying the fruits of his discoveries in Maine to the oils of Gloucester's more familiar environs. His new style appeared to meet with popular and critical favor. Of one ill-fated Gloucester painting done in 1856, the local paper later recounted that

the Lane painting of Gloucester . . . was burned at the time the Town Hall, on the present site of City hall, was destroyed by fire. This painting was considered by far the best of the several paintings by Fitz H. Lane and was a view of Gloucester from Rocky Neck at the time Mr. Lane painted it in 1856. From this painting Mr. Lane had finished a number of lithographs which were sold at a very low price. This did not bring to Mr. Lane much ready money and he was somewhat disappointed so he mounted several of these on canvas, painted them in oil and sold them to several of his friends for $25 and there are a number of these at present held in Gloucester and valued very highly.[6]

However, several major works of Gloucester from 1857 have survived. One of the most interesting is *Three Master on the Gloucester Railway* (*Ill. 71*), painted originally as a shop sign for John Trask's paint store at Burnham Bros. Railway. The *Cape Ann Advertiser* carried a note about the work just after its completion:

PRETTY SIGN—If our readers wish to see something pretty, let them take a walk down to Burnham Bros. Railway and take a peep at the new sign recently hung out over the paint shop of Mr. John Trask. It is a painting on canvas $4\frac{1}{2}$ feet by 5 executed by Fitz H. Lane, Esq., representing a view of Burnham Bros. Railways, the wharf and stores adjoining. The front view represents the "ways" with a ship and schooner receiving a coat of paint. The workshop and counting-room of Burnham Bros. and the buildings of Mr. Joseph Shepherd, together with the old Parrott and Caswell houses are plainly visible. In the background, a partial view of the residence of Capt. Frederick Norwood on Spring street, the Universalist church on Elm street, Capt. Isaac Somes' residence on Pleasant street and several other buildings on Prospect St. The view is taken from Rocky Neck and makes a very pretty picture.[7]

Another newspaper article noted:

The ship which is shown on the railway is the California, a noted craft owned by the late George H. Rogers, and engaged in the Surinam trade, and which was driven out of the harbor in one of the worst storms of the century, January 18, 1857, together with the lightering schooner Nile. Three men were on board the crafts, which were warped together, one of whom was Mr. Rogers' factotum, Michael O'Maley, father of Police Officer Charles O'Maley, but fortunately the crafts drifted ashore on the beach at Scituate and the men escaped drowning.[8]

The picture lacks much of the detailing seen in most Lane works, no doubt because Lane was conscious of painting on a large scale an image that was to be viewed from below and at some distance. The design of the picture relies largely on the play of various near-geometric forms; for example, the cubic shapes of the buildings contrast with the pyramidal grouping of the three vessels. Similarly, Lane alternates linear and planar elements here, such as wall surfaces and ship rigging. In a composition that could have become monotonously balanced, he places the stern of the three-master very slightly to the right of center and, making the vessel not quite perpendicular to the spectator. Given its function, the painting reconciles the sense of three-dimensional volume with surface pattern surprisingly well.

Also in 1857, Lane made the drawing *Field Beach,* with the notation "Painting for Joe and Caroline Stevens." Shortly after the completion of an oil from the drawing (*Ill. 72*), he wrote to the Stevenses to tell them about it:

Since writing you last I have painted but one picture worth talking about and that one I intend for you if you should be pleased with it. It is a view of the beach between Stage Fort and Steep bank, including Hovey's Hill and residence, fresh water cove, and the point of land with the lone pine tree. Fessenden's house likewise comes into the picture. The effect is a mid-day light, with a cloudy sky, a patch of sunlight is thrown across the beach and the breaking waves. An old vessel lies stranded on the beach with two or three figures. There are a few vessels in the distance and the Field rocks likewise show at the left of the picture. I think you will be pleased with this picture, for it is a very picturesque scene especially the beach, as there are many rocks which come in to destroy the monotony of a plain sand beach, and I have so arranged the light and shade that the effect I think is very good indeed; however, you will be better able to judge of that when you see it.[9]

Moving his vantage point out a little into the center of Gloucester Harbor, Lane next drew a section of the shoreline adjacent to Field Beach. One drawing, *Stage Rocks,* was "sketched from a lumber loaded vessel by F. H. Lane for a painting ordered by John J. Piper. Another picture afterward painted from the same for Capt. Frank Gale and wife." A second drawing, titled *Gloucester Outer Harbor,* was carefully squared off to permit the accurate translation of details to the larger-scaled oils; while a third drawing of the scene served as the basis for a "picture painted . . . for Mrs. William F. Davis." At least two closely related oils of *Stage Rocks and Western Shore of Gloucester Outer Harbor* are extant (*Plate VIII; Ill. 73*). The larger version (*Plate VIII*) is described in the same letter of 1857 to Stevens in which he mentions the *Field Beach* painting. The fragment of the letter begins in mid-sentence:

> . . . will fully appreciate all that I have done in my garden, in ornamenting it with flowers and plants, Rustic Arbours and Statues. . . . I yesterday made a sketch of Stage Fort and the surounding [*sic*] scenery, from the water. Piper has given me an order for a picture from this point of view, to be treated as a sunset [*Plate VIII*]. I shall try to make something out of it, but it will require some management, as there is no foreground but water and vessels. One o'clock, it is very hot, the glass indicates 84° in my room, with the windows open and a light breeze from the east. This is the warmest day.[10]

The resulting painting captures something of the heat and lassitude that Lane describes. As for the problem of an empty foreground, he partially fills it with four vessels, arranged in a zig-zag relationship across the picture surface. The positions of these boats, which suggest an oscillating movement toward and away from the shore, echo the curving line of beaches and promonotories, and the pattern made by clouds and shadows reflected in the water also undulates in gentle wavelike design across the canvas. In fact, the problem of the foreground was not a very serious one for Lane; he clearly

did not seek to fill any area of the painting with objects or figures, as the
large expanse of water and sky make apparent. Rather, his foremost concern
here was the light and the time of day. With masterful control of color, Lane
moves from the intense yellows and oranges of the setting sun at the right
across through increasingly darker shades of grayish pinks in the central
clouds to a touch of purple on the distant horizon at the left. At the top of the
canvas a deep blue fades gradually into the paler colors at the horizon, while
the water surface is a myriad of small touches of pure pinks, yellows, greens,
and blues laid side by side in an almost impressionistic technique. All in all,
it is one of Lane's supreme achievements, in which the presence of light is
virtually an embodiment of reverence. That is to say, Lane's treatment of
light in his Maine and Gloucester views is evidence less of a meteorological
than of a spiritual condition. Such clear, radiant light in many of his later
paintings is a statement of optimism and plenitude; parallels can be found
in the work of several contemporaries at this moment in American art. Most
notable are such works as William Sidney Mount's *Cider Making* of 1851
and George Caleb Bingham's *Fur Traders Descending the Missouri* of 1845
(both Metropolitan Museum, New York), in which haloes of light and atmosphere reflect the artist's affection for, and confidence in, their native landscape and character.[11]

The second painting of *Stage Rocks* (*Ill. 73*) is considerably simplified as
compared with the first, now depicting the scene in broad sunlight. Lane
shows a more head-on and therefore a shorter extent of the shore line. Only
two major vessels are in the foreground here, and the range of colors in this
midday scene is naturally reduced. Still, it retains the calm restraint of the
larger version. Moving back to shore, Lane did another view of the same
rocks (now Stage Fort Park), once more in the quiet of late afternoon (*Ill.
74*). As is increasingly characteristic of his later work, only two small figures
are present in the scene. The prominent personalities are the rounded boulders and rock outcroppings, the soft textures of the silhouetted trees, and, always, the light, here as forceful in the shadowy reflections as on illuminated
surfaces.

The area had historical significance, for it was here that Champlain was
said to have landed at the beginning of the seventeenth century. In fact, on
the drawing preparatory to the *Stage Rocks* oil is the inscription "Perhaps
from this sketch Lane made his painting to represent the 'Landing at Cape
Anne' [*sic*]." Lane began another painting of this shore in 1858, evidently
with some historical details or figures included in the view, according to a

long and interesting correspondence published about it in the Gloucester paper:

I cannot close this rambling article without some reference to a picture, which evidently Mr. Lane was engaged in painting in the summer of 1858 to be called the "Landing at Cape Anne, 1623," a picture inspired by a visit to him in January of that year by J. Wingate Thornton, the author of the very interesting and valuable historical book, "The Landing at Cape Anne," published originally in 1854. The following letters seem to me of sufficient interest to publish in full.

20 Court St., Boston, Jan. 6, 1858.

Dear Sir:—Willingly do my thoughts revert to the half hour passed awhile since in your pleasant study at Gloucester and today while adding a note for a new edition of the "Landing at Cape Anne," the idea of a sketch or picture of the locality as it was in the year 1624 again comes to mind. . . .

If the interest of the subject shall lead you, at leisure hours, to ponder over this scene and its incidents and to picture it on paper, or canvas, I shall be highly gratified in having been the means of thus honorably identifying your professional skill and fame with a leading epoch in American national history.

It will be multiplied by the engraver, adorn our volumes of history, and find its way into school books.

Perhaps in a year another edition of the "Landing at Cape Anne," will be ready for the press, and I shall be highly pleased to have the proposed picture engraved for its frontispiece.

I shall be glad to hear from you and am with great respect and regard,

Yours,
J. Wingate Thornton.

20 Court St., Boston,
20 July, 1858

Mr. Lane—

My Dear Sir:—Your letter of welcome news that the picture of "the landing at Cape Anne" is finished took me by surprise for I feared that the difficulty at finding contemporary details especially in naval architecture might have discouraged you from the attempt. Mr. Babson's opinion of your success is very flattering and I am eager to see you, your picture of a scene which ought to be, and, I believe, will be, familiar to every school boy. . . .

With great respect and regard,
Yours,
J. Wingate Thornton.

20 Court St., Boston.
31 July, 1858.

Fitz H. Lane, Gloucester.

My Dear Sir:—Since my pleasant visit at your studio I have been studying your picture and one or two ideas are suggested, which I communicate.

1st. Among the items of the "plantation," several cattle were sent over:—these indicate the plan, the idea of permanency of agriculture and they may be introduced into your picture to add to its historical fidelity:—the cattle being as Essential to the picture as the ships are in which you have been so successful.

2nd. Introduce Roger Conant, as the principal figure, he being the soul, the head of the Enterprise. This will give action, life, to the scene and in no wise affect the truth of the picture, but as it is essential to its historical integrity completeness.

Yours very truly,
J. Wingate Thornton.[12]

The work has since disappeared.

Other Gloucester drawings of interest from this period included a distant panorama of the town from Steepbank, Samuel Sawyer's homestead.

By 1857 Lane was financially secure enough to be listed in the town tax rolls, for on September 5 the *Gloucester Telegraph* noted that "the Assessors of this town have completed their valuation, and issued their tax lists for the current year. . . . Below we give a list of the persons, estates, and firms who are taxed $25 and upwards. . . . Fitz H. Lane, $36.70." That year T. J. Herring lent *Manchester Harbor* by Lane to the annual Boston Athenaeum exhibition. All told, 1857 saw Lane at the height of his career: recognized, happy, prosperous, and active.

CHAPTER EIGHT
AMONG THE BEST OF HIS WORKS

The last phase of Lane's work begins in the late 1850's. It is for the most part characterized by thin applications of paint, transparent effects of light, and de-emphasis of detail and action. One exception is *New York Yacht Club Regatta* of 1857 (Shelburne Museum, Shelburne, Vt.)—William Bradford painted an almost identical scene at the same time (Edgartown Yacht Club, Edgartown, Mass.)[1]—although even this type of relatively dramatic subject Lane adapted to his late style of understatement. Among the best examples of this evocative manner are the several oils that he did at this time of Gloucester and Boston harbors. For instance, *Gloucester Harbor at Sunset* (*Ill. 75*) is an intense example of Lane's unique combination of crystalline drawing and luminously transparent atmosphere. His views of *Boston Harbor* (Collection Bronson Trevor, New York; and *Ill. 76*) are more complex compositions for which he found equally tranquil and lucid solutions. Whether subconsciously or not, Lane seems to have developed in these last years of his career a preference for scenes of dusk rather than dawn. Where earlier, *Bear Island* at sunrise or *Southwest Harbor* at midday were metaphorical images respectively of expectation and serene satisfaction, these pictures done in Lane's own old age may be thought of as expressions of culmination and fulfillment.

Belonging to this group are less identifiable views, such as *Vessels off the Massachusetts Coast* (Collection Dr. Dallas Pratt, New York)—similar to *Gloucester Harbor at Sunset* although a little more loosely organized—and *Sailing off Cape Ann* (Collection Charles D. Childs, Boston), a scene of rough waters with an expansive openness. One of the Mount Desert pictures of 1859 was described in the Gloucester paper by its owner: "I am fortunate in owning a very delightful picture painted by Mr. Lane of a sunset scene off Mt. Desert, Maine, which Mr. Lane gave to my aunt in 1859 as a wedding present. This picture will in my judgment compare most favorably as among the best of his work." [2] Two other Maine pictures from 1859 are small oils of the *Stevens Homestead* in Castine, shown surrounded by leafy trees and flowering gardens (private collection and Collection Mr. and Mrs. Andrew Wyeth, Cushing, Maine).

A good indication of Lane's preferences in subject matter at this time are the titles of the pictures he sent to the national exhibitions: He called two of his paintings for sale in 1859 at the Boston Athenaeum *Sunset in the Bay,* and a third, *Sunset After a Storm.* In 1860 he was painting again in Penobscot Bay, Maine, where he did one of his most poetic twilight pictures, *Lumber Schooners at Evening on Penobscot Bay (Ill. 77).* By contrast, he created a dramatic image in *Schooners Before Approaching Storm (Off Owl's Head) (Ill. 78),* in which the stark white of the sails and masts is silhouetted against the blacks of the gathering storm clouds. Its brooding severity suggests that Lane might have made contact that year with Martin Johnson Heade for the first time. Although Heade's *Approaching Storm, Beach near Newport (Ill. 81)* is thought to date from a few years later, he had already painted a similarly threatening scene, probably off Cape Ann, titled *Storm Clouds on the Coast* (Farnsworth Museum, Rockland, Maine), in 1859. Moreover, he also exhibited paintings at the Boston Athenaeum in at least two years when Lane's work was there, 1857 and 1859. Certainly, the threatening calm in Lane's *Storm (off Owl's Head)* is new in his work and would appear to draw on elements that were already present in Heade's art. In turn, this striking vision of nature's forces at sea may well have crystallized the younger Heade's emerging image of surrealistic power. Probably Lane's work was the picture listed as *Approaching Storm* that he offered for sale in the 1860 Athenaeum exhibition.

Something more of Lane's relationship to his contemporaries may be understood by comparing his work both to his known followers and to others working in a style close to his. Two views of *Norman's Woe* in 1862 (*Ills. 79* and *80*), for which he had done a preliminary drawing the previous year, are typical of his late style. While the extreme clarity of forms and excessive care with such details as the flowers in the larger work (*Ill. 79*) have a visual power similar to Heade's landscapes, the second, smaller oil possesses a superior refinement and evocativeness. In this he lessens the emphasis on the figures and the sailboat, by moving them to one side, and gives up the charming but distracting details of flowers and wrecked hull; he also eliminates the ripples on the water surface, reduces the number and size of the rocks, and everywhere softens the contrasts of light and dark. As a consequence, the painting takes on a unity and legibility that is new, again directing our attention to the perception of luminosity.

The painting *Gloucester Harbor and Dolliver's Neck* (*Ill. 82*) by Lane's pupil Mary B. Mellen, only recently identified as her work, reveals how close she came to imitating his style. She was born in Sterling, Massachusetts, and early became interested in painting. Her first training in art came from a boarding school instructor. When she married the Reverend C. W. Mellen, they moved to Gloucester, where he was the Universalist minister, and sometime during the 1850's she became Lane's pupil, both copying his works and attempting originals of her own.

Occasionally, Lane sufficiently trusted her abilities to collaborate with her on a painting. At least one oil, the unusual circular canvas *Maine Coastal View* (private collection), is signed by both Mellen and Lane. She became proficient enough to receive praise in her own right from the press. In this regard an amusing incident, probably apocryphal, has been recorded about the teacher and his pupil:

> Her copy of Lane's "On the Lee Shore" has elicited the warm encomiums of the press. One editor remarked, "An old sea-dog, in looking at it yesterday, exclaimed, 'Them anchors yer only hope!'" and added, "Mrs. Mellen is so faithful in the copies of her master, that even an expert might take them for originals. Indeed, an anecdote is related of her, which will exemplify her power in this direction. She had just completed a copy of one of Mr. Lane's pictures when he called at her residence to see it. The copy and the original were brought down from the studio together, and the master, much to the amusement of those present, was unable to tell which was his own, and which was the pupil's." [3]

From looking at her oil *Gloucester Harbor and Dolliver's Neck,* it is not immediately apparent how it differs from Lane's work. The clues to her style—and weaknesses in comparison to Lane—are the repetitive treatment of the waves, the lack of assurance in drawing rigging and other linear details, and the general softness of volumes, particularly rocks and the hulls of vessels. By contrast, how convincingly Lane's boats sit in the water, how surely his wind fills their sails, how varied are his details, and how crystalline is his air. While this particular canvas is signed on the reverse "Painted by M. B. Mellen after F. H. Lane, 1870," others have not been so explicitly marked and thus can cause problems for the careless eye.

D. Jerome Elwell's copies after Lane are equally challenging. One was his re-creation of Lane's 1856 view of Gloucester burned in the 1864 fire. After Lane's death, Elwell also "touched upon" several of his pictures (*Ill. 34*). Others in the Elwell family had artistic ambitions, and as a boy Jerome began to make pencil copies after works by other artists. Much younger than Lane, he completed high school in Gloucester in the last years of Lane's life and shortly after went to Antwerp to study. This travel was made possible by the generosity of Samuel Sawyer, who was also a patron of Lane in the 1860's. During the 1870's, Elwell traveled around the Low Countries and elsewhere in Europe, at one time (it was said) sharing a studio with Whistler in Venice.[4] Like Lane, he cultivated a taste for twilight and moonlight effects.

Elwell's style tended to be harsher and his colors more metallic; in fact, the differences in manner between Elwell and Lane directly reflect the differences in their generations. Lane belonged to the first half of the nineteenth century, with its unquestioning optimism and its self-conscious nationalism. By contrast, Elwell's career embraced much of the second half of the century, and there is a corresponding Victorian fussiness and embellishment, as well as a flavor of internationalism, about his work. Some of this may be seen in his view of *Gloucester from Dolliver's Neck* (*Ill. 83*). While the subject and composition owe an obvious debt to Lane, whom Elwell very much admired but probably never studied under, most of the background is executed with a loose and flashy handling of paint quite unlike Lane. Furthermore, some of Elwell's details, such as his clouds, indicate an unimaginative arbitrariness; his strident hot colors, too, contrast with Lane's cool and misty tones. One can readily see why to Elwell's eye Lane's pictures seemed weak and thin and in need of touching up or strengthening.

Besides Jerome and his brother Kilby Elwell and Mary Mellen, there were others not quite so well known who worked in Lane's manner, indicating the high regard in which his achievements were held. For example, Henry J. Pierce painted an exact replica of *Ships in Ice off Ten Pound Island* (Shore Galleries, Boston), and G. Merchant, Jr., copied Lane's *Smart Blow* in 1863 (location unknown). An oil, *Fishermen at Sea,* by James Hamilton (Shelburne Museum, Shelburne, Vt.) was at one time thought to be Lane's work —in fact, someone added his signature to it. Meanwhile, Lane had a noticeable influence on the work of several New Bedford painters, including William Bradford, Albert Van Beest, and William A. Wall. These men went back and forth between New Bedford and Boston several times during the 1850's, and they could have met Lane in either place.[5]

More intriguing are the similarities between Lane's mature work and that of painters in the second generation of the Hudson River School. Compare

The Western Shore with Norman's Woe (*Ill. 80*) with John F. Kensett's *Shrewsbury River, New Jersey* of 1859 (*Ill. 84*). At just about the same moment both artists, along with Church, Heade, and others, had arrived at a translucent, luminous style. Kensett also prefers here the strong horizontal format, the evocative emptiness of space, the controlled contrasts of light and dark silhouettes, and the suffusing aura of clear sunlight. His travels may or may not have put him in touch with Lane personally: Throughout the late 1840's and the 1850's he traveled extensively in central and coastal New England. But whether or not they ever met, it is not surprising that his style and subject matter shared characteristics with Lane: Both men had had early training as graphic artists, and their manners of expression would naturally reflect a sense of line and tonal values. Furthermore, Kensett, Lane, Heade, Church, and others were exhibiting and working together in New York City or Boston, and they would probably have taken the opportunity to see their own and each other's work on view at the American Art-Union or the Boston Athenaeum. (A summary of a few of the pertinent dates during this period is useful: Shown at the Athenaeum in 1857 were works by Lane, Bradford, Van Beest, and Heade; in 1859, the work of Lane, Heade, Kensett, Gifford, Bradford, and Bierstadt. At the Art-Union Lane and Church were exhibited together in 1847, 1848, 1849 and 1850.)

Lane continued through 1862 to develop greater openness and lucidity in his style. Notable in this regard are his oils *Ipswich Bay* (Museum of Fine Arts, Boston) and *Coffin's Beach* (Collection Martha Low, Gloucester, Mass.), both sunrise scenes without figures. An interesting drawing from the same year was *Fremont's Encampment at the Loaf, West Gloucester,* from which "Lane made a painting . . . and presented it to Mrs. Fremont."

Unique in its inspiration is Lane's *"Dream Painting"* of 1862 (*Ill. 86*). In a letter attached to the back of the canvas Lane recounted the circumstances of its inspiration:

This picture, the property of John S. Webber, Esq., Collector of the Port and District of Gloucester, was suggested to the artist by a dream. Sometime last fall while lying in bed asleep, a richly furnished room was presented to my imagination. Upon the wall my attention was attracted to a picture which I have here endeavored to reproduce. The dream was very vivid and on awakening I retained it in memory for a long time. The effect was so beautiful in the dream that I determined to attempt its reproduction, and this picture is the result. The drawing is very correct, but the effect falls far short of what I saw, and it would be impossible to convey to canvas such gorgeous and brilliant coloring as was presented to me. This picture, however, will give to the beholder some faint idea of the ideal.[6]

During the summer of 1862 Lane had had a falling out with his brother-in-law, Ignatius Winter. Lane had lived with his sister Sarah and Winter in the old stone house for nearly twelve years, and a cause unknown to us now created sufficient ill-feeling for Lane to move out briefly. In fact, he was a guest at the home of his Gloucester friend Dr. Davidson (now the Sawyer Free Library) when he had the dream. Early the next morning he presented a preliminary pencil study to Mrs. Davidson, and later, during the winter of 1862–3, he painted the oil for her husband for fifty dollars. The drawing is a crisply finished work, while the painting possesses an over-all tonality of golden-brown, with the hazy light falling on the hull of the vessel and filling the undefined background behind.

In addition, Lane also completed the spacious *Merchantmen off Boston Harbor* (Shelburne Museum, Shelburne, Vt.) and the crystalline painting of *Owl's Head, Penobscot Bay, Maine* from the beach on Monroe Island (*Ill. 41*). Though he would return to Maine one final time in 1863, this is his last known view of the head—an apt culmination of his many earlier images. Even as he approached the age of sixty, the Maine coast summoned him for fresh explorations and new looks at familiar places. But age had made its mark on the artist, as the late photograph of him (*Ill. 85*) intimates. It is a typical *carte de visite* and may have served as the basis for his occasional self-portraits, one of which Edward Lane later owned and another of which the artist bequeathed to Mary Mellen.

Lane's last paintings were among his most poignant and beautiful, and his pace of production in 1863 and 1864 did not noticeably slacken. During August, 1863, he got at least as far as Maine, where he made his drawing *Looking up Portland Harbor* and ruled off the photograph of the *Steamer "Harvest Moon"* (*Ill. 50*). This use of photography marks an important element in American art at this time. One need hardly mention that American photography as an independent artistic medium was coming into its own in the hands of such men as Matthew Brady and Alexander Gardner. Their stark images of the War between the States were appearing in the very year that the *Harvest Moon* was photographed. It is now known that such nineteenth-century European painters as Delacroix, Courbet, and Manet often made use of daguerreotypes or photographs in their art, but much less attention has been paid to the role of this art form in American painting after mid-century. As we have seen, its capacity for measuring and objectifying the visual world found a sympathetic use in Lane's work. But photography was also a sign of a more pervasive American characteristic—a continuing fascination with science. A number of American artists, from Charles Willson Peale and Samuel F. B. Morse to William Rimmer, have shown equal interests in art and science. In the second half of the nineteenth century, such painters as William Bradford, Thomas Eakins, and possibly Winslow Homer made use of photography in their work. Although photography may have introduced a new form of realism, fundamentally it reinforced the recurring American penchant for the physical and the practical. That it came to flourish in a century concerned with the nature of seeing is understandable. More provocative, perhaps, is the link that might be made to another nineteenth-century preoccupation, that of exploring the nature of time, both biological and geological. This was a century fascinated with the age of the earth and the evolution of man. Photography brought many of these concerns together for the artist. Especially as a process of vision, it lends us insight into Lane's view of the world. His paintings, seemingly so close to photographs in their realism, were, paradoxically, images of time at once stopped and without duration. His landscapes look both measured and measureless.

To the east of Portland, he cruised with Stevens to Christmas Cove, where he did at least two oils (private collection, and *Ill. 87*). In both he has set two small rocky islands to either side of the center of the canvas. Maintaining his subtle feeling for balances, he contrasts the aging pines on the left with the upright verticals of the schooner's masts on the right. Holding the two sides of the composition together is a bird perched on a rock at the center. Like a late vision of Turner, Lane draws the eye directly into the incandescent axis of light at dawn. Thus do we confront directly its blaze of glory for a final time. Truly, light as physical and metaphysical presence has become the ordering element in his painting.

He went on to paint a moonlight view of a place visited earlier, *Indian Bar Cove, Brooksville, Maine (Ills. 88 and 89)*. If we think too rigidly that Lane in the latter part of his career had become a lonely recluse, preferring to avoid the company of all but Stevens, these two charming scenes of fishing parties should temper our view. The figures are among the most attractive Lane painted, and the daylight version has an intimacy and warmth often missing in more formal (and larger) canvases. Only in the moonlight scene is there any intimation of that romantic nostalgia that recurred more frequently at the end of his life, as it also did in Allston's and Salmon's late paintings. There is a brief hint, too, of a weakening in the handling of certain details, such as the rather hard patterns of clouds and somewhat strong yellow for the moon's reflection. The unobtrusive harmony of *Moonlight Fishing Scene* (*Half Way Rock*) of a decade earlier (*Ill. 62*) has now dissipated slightly. Yet Lane's personal touch is readily observed when compared to *Moonlight Scene: Gloucester Harbor,* probably by Mary Mellen (*Ill. 90*). This picture was formerly attributed to Lane, but like the earlier Mellen-Lane comparison (*Ills. 80* and *82*), this also displays her distinctive hand.[7] There is a particular hardness to the surface of the water and to the boats, typical of her copies. The drawing of the rigging is weak in places, and the over-all color has a metallic and unvaried quality. Because it comes so close to Lane's known work and is at the same time unsigned, it typifies the problems of attribution that sometimes attend discussion of Lane's work.

Another Maine work of 1863 is *Lumber Schooner in a Storm* (*Ill. 91*), the culminating example of the dramatic type of painting in Lane's career. Once again, man is alone at sea, confronting and dealing with nature's forces as best he can. Although an action subject, it has few of the story-telling details of his early style. The schooner is set back from the foreground, adding to the detachment with which we view her fate, and the men are small and unrecognizable. Appropriate to the vigor of the subject, Lane paints the churning waves with active brushstrokes and builds up the paint thickly, especially on the white crests. Just as his glazes were technically suited to his scenes of pale, transient light, here the thicker and more active application of paint is physically equated to the image represented. His compositional solution again employs a slight asymmetry in the placement of the vessel to the left of center, yet moving to the right, and he focuses attention on the precarious work of the men taking in the sails by silhouetting the topmost dark figure against a single white cloud.

This intense experience of nature, so much a part of Lane's experience in Maine, was equally part of Frederic Church's painting at the time. The evidence from exhibition records, stylistic comparisons, and biographical information has already suggested several points of contact between Lane and Church. Not the least of them was their shared interest in the coastal wilderness of Maine; after the exhibition of Lane's *Twilight on the Kennebec* in 1849, both he and Church were painting not far apart at Mount Desert during at least four summers of the 1850's. Church's *Sunrise off the Maine Coast* (*Storm off Mount Desert*) (*Ill. 92*) places him there in 1863 as well. The technique of his painting and his feeling for the subject show how close together the two came during this period. Church went on to a much different career in the second half of the century, but the present comparison illuminates a broader vision shared by a number of artists. Thus, from a heightened

awareness of various individual styles we may with increasing confidence define what is clearly a period style: compositions largely devoted to sky; transparent and radiant effects of light, often emphasized by contrasts of dark,
silhouetted shapes in the landscape; and the meaning of nature expressed as
much through the intangible and spiritual as through the tangible and physical. Between about 1855 and 1875, similar examples of this so-called luminist
manner can be seen in the work of Heade, Church, Kensett, Gifford, Whittredge, Bierstadt, Inness, and others of their generation. It is important to un-
understand not only Lane's own growth but also to place his work in the
larger context of American art.

Besides his activities in Maine, Lane also managed to paint ship portraits,
such as the *Brig "Antelope" in Boston Harbor* (Museum of Fine Arts, Boston), which concluded a long line of Boston Harbor views in his career. A
similar harbor scene appears in *Ship "Starlight" in the Fog* (*Ill. 93*), although
the location is not identifiable. His handling of the sun breaking through the
hazy mist again recalls Church's *Sunrise off the Maine Coast* of about the
same date. The early work of William Bradford, before his trips to the Arctic
in the late 1860's and the 1870's, also indicates a thorough awareness of Lane's
painting (*Ill. 94*). Not only Bradford's general composition but also the care
in defining sails and rigging, as well as the treatment of atmospheric light,
may well derive their inspiration from Lane.

CHAPTER NINE
DEATH OF LANE THE PAINTER

Lane's final paintings are supreme achievements, images of acceptance and reverence. Technically, they were produced in the artist's familiar manner of careful pencil studies and delicate balancing of forms in space, and the subjects are all familiar Gloucester landmarks. His life and his art had come full circle.

But at least two of these works were not merely culminations of a style; they were also fresh and original in subject. During the summer of 1863 Lane went inland on Cape Ann, and near the marshy wetlands surrounding the Annisquam River he made several pencil drawings. From two of the sketches came a pair of surprising landscapes, *Riverdale* (*Plate IX*) and *Babson and Ellery Houses, Gloucester* (*Ill. 98*). For an artist so consistently and narrowly thought of as a marine painter, these two pictures are revelations. In reviewing Lane's prior career, however, one soon recognizes familiar isolated notes, which here emerge together with a new strength. For example, the broad view of the landscape and the gentle horizontal curve of the foreground in *Riverdale* appeared earlier in his *Castine from Fort George* (*Ill. 38*); the fresh greens of a summer landscape were the animating presence in *The Sawyer Homestead* (Sawyer Free Library, Gloucester; preliminary drawing, *Ill. 56*) and *Gloucester from Brookbank* (*Ill. 55*); the rolling slopes of a distant hillside seen against the sky had predecessors in his paintings of Blue Hill, Camden, and Mount Desert (*Plates V* and *VII*); and the soft, caressing sunlight came from a lifetime of study.

A more immediate source for this unusual pair of pictures at this point in Lane's career appears to have been the work of Martin Johnson Heade. Heade was peripatetic, a compulsive traveler, who had studios at one time or another in various cities along the East Coast of the United States, in the Midwest,

84

and on the West Coast. He also visited Europe twice and painted in South
America several times. During the late 1850's he had worked occasionally in
New England, painting coastal scenes in Rhode Island and Maine. It is known
that during 1861 he was briefly at work in the Studio Building in Boston.
During the next year he painted the first of his many scenes in the hay
marshes. Among the areas he was to frequent irregularly were the marsh
fields of Newburyport and Ipswich, just to the north of Cape Ann. During
the summer of 1863 Heade and Lane may well have met again or seen each
other's paintings; some of their pictures (for example, of Ipswich) are markedly alike at this time.

In *Riverdale* (*Plate IX*) one notes a number of aspects that would seem to
derive from Heade's style as exemplified in such a work as his *Sunrise on the
Marshes* (*Ill. 95*), painted in the same year. Notable are Lane's predominantly
blue and green tonalities here (which appear in another Heade, *Spring
Showers in the Connecticut Valley* of 1868 [Museum of Fine Arts, Boston]);
the carefully rounded clumps of rocks, trees, and haycart played off against
the lateral lines of the roadway and the horizon; and the relative de-emphasis
of the foreground—a direction Lane was moving in, but already a special
characteristic of Heade's compositions. In turn, what might Heade have
borrowed from a look at Lane's painting? Two details here strike the eye
particularly: the glowing central axis of sunlight and the fisherman in the
foreground who wears a bright red shirt. Some sort of personal exchange
may have taken place as early as 1860, as comparison of the storm scenes by
the two painters has already suggested (*Ills. 78* and *81*). But the stylistic link
seems to be even stronger by 1863. When one recalls that Church and Heade
were longtime friends, and that there were a number of possible connections
between Lane and Church, some sort of three-way association is a convincing
likelihood.

Lane made an unusual number of preparatory drawings for *Riverdale,* and
several of them are ruled off into quadrants, a practice used on the Portland
photograph of the same year (*Ill. 50*). He began with the panoramic *View
Across the Marsh and Millpond in Town Parish,* a drawing that is essentially
complete in rendering the distant town and landscape as they appear in the
oil. A second drawing (*Ill. 96*) views the Town Parish from another vantage
point and attempts to deal with the same components of landscape and
buildings at closer range and in different relationship to each other. As if to
explore, and thereby understand fully, all aspects of the scene, Lane undertook a third drawing. *Fence with Landscape* (*Ill. 97*) is clearly a detail from
one of the more comprehensive views and a minor part of the final painting,

where it appears curving away behind the stone fence to the left of center. Yet by signing this extraordinary little work Lane himself has confirmed what is evident in looking at it: it possesses all the integrity of a finished work of art, with a remarkable feeling of both intimacy and spaciousness. As part of a sequence of drawings, this sketch illustrates Lane's process of testing every element in his picture. In this way the resolution of each part makes possible the harmonious order of the whole.

Actually, the third drawing is a microcosm of the finished picture. Not only do the presence of fence and landscape anticipate the final subject, but the gentle tension of forms carries over from drawing to painting. The placement of the fenceposts anticipates the haycart and boulders; moreover, the right-hand fencepost occupies approximately the same position, just to the right of center, as the haycart. As the fencepost and rail represent a visual joining of vertical and horizontal, so the haycart is placed at a similar juncture with the crossing roadway. Lane makes us conscious in drawing and painting alike of the strong linear elements (fence rail and roadway) moving laterally across the foreground, in contrast to the planar pull into space of the meadow behind. Taken together, the picture is as well conceived and composed as any of his marines. Just as he often used quasi-geometric designs, such as pyramidal groupings, for placing vessels in a harbor, so here he organizes the haycart at the center of a flattened **X**, along whose crossed arms lie the clumps of rocks and trees. Just as he frequently defined spatial recession across the surface of water by means of alternating horizontal bands of light and shadow, here he alternates the light silhouettes of cart and rocks in the foreground with the dark patterns of trees in the middleground and the sunny landscape once again in the distance. In a harbor view, he habitually left an open corridor of water down the center of the painting, through which the eye might read easily from the foreground back to the far shoreline (see *Plate III; Ill. 76*). In *Riverdale* the eye moves easily along the track of the cart through the foreground, then through the fence gate, and finally through the framing dark foliage into the broadly lit, open field beyond.

For a procedure sounding so methodical, the finished painting is not impersonal. Partly, this is due to the inclusion of two small figures, a man driving the cart and a woman walking along the road. More profoundly, though, the warmth and unaffected naturalness of Lane's treatment of the landscape denotes an ambience of affection and personal care.

The preliminary drawing for *Babson and Ellery Houses* is a highly finished one; apparently, Lane made no other studies. Again in this quiet picture of familiar houses and flourishing gardens (*Ill. 98*) there are hints of earlier works, notably the very early town views in Boston (*Ill. 3*) and the 1859 oils of the Stevens houses in Castine. There were more immediate predecessors in Lane's drawings of the two houses prepared in 1860 for John J. Babson's *History of Gloucester*. The artist's consistent delight in different textures is present, as always, but the painting is unmistakably a later work in the over-riding attention given to light. Here, in a daring decision, he turns over almost three-quarters of the canvas to the pale pink glow of the sky. The two houses prominently shown in the oil are still standing today.

For a painter whose expression in art so often stated the human presence implicitly rather than explicitly, it is appropriate that the last dated oils are without figures. The subject to which he devoted extended time and effort during his last active winter was Brace's Rock. On the northeast side of Eastern Point, this large rocky ledge sticks out dangerously into the waters approaching Cape Ann. As such, "in the days of sail it was one of the worst hazards anywhere on the New England coast."[1] Lane's paintings titled *Brace's Rock, Eastern Point, Gloucester (Plate X; Ill. 101)* intimate something of the danger in the stark outlines of the isolated rocks and the presence of a wrecked hull. Even though the moment he chooses to paint is the calm of a soft sunset, the subtle reminders of human misfortune add a deeper meaning to this scene of romantic nostalgia.

A work by Heade of this same date indicates further association between the two painters. *The Stranded Boat (Ill. 99)* is thought to have been painted by Heade somewhere on the Rhode Island coast, although it is impossible to identify the location precisely, and its format would seem to owe a strong debt to Lane's painting. For Heade it is an uncharacteristic composition, with its strong stress on the foreground; one's attention focuses on the beached sailboat as the primary subject, strikingly unlike his more typical marsh scene *(Ill. 95)* in which he leads the eye back quickly toward the salt hay-stacks near the horizon. If *Riverdale* represents what Lane drew from Heade, then *The Stranded Boat* illustrates the reverse. Heade's boat has just been pulled up by someone out sailing; a figure fishes off the distant point, while others drift in boats through the fog. Lane's work, by contrast, implies tragedy since the boat has been abandoned for some time. Actually, the surreal clarity and vacuum-like air of Lane's painting come closer to Heade's later paintings of storms approaching over Narragansett Bay (for example, *Ill. 81*). The distinctive aspect of *Brace's Rock* is its assertion of time and duration. Where time in Heade's work is evident only in the actions of the moment, Lane's images, on the surface, indicate a longer history and, more profoundly, suggest a transcendence or suspension of time.

Lane's first drawing of the area was from the south looking north over the point and across Brace's Cove. It is a sweeping view, taking in a wide section of the shoreline. Significantly, the point of the ledge extends completely across the composition, whereas the final oil gives the eye a clear path out to the infinite horizon. Lane was not fully satisfied with the angle of this particular view, as Stevens's note on the drawing hints: "Painting ordered from the entire sketch by Mrs. S. G. Rogers of Roxbury. Shortly before his death Lane prepared a canvas 22 x 36 for it, and that was all!" He did proceed, however, with another drawing (*Ill. 100*) which he found suitable, so much so that during the following winter he painted no less than five oils from the sketch, of which at least three are known to exist today. This second drawing views the cove from the north and now stresses the rock at the center as the major subject of attention. In the final painting (*Plate X*), Lane moves his vantage point even closer, eliminating much of the foreground beach and tightly foreshortening the dark point of rocks extending into the water on the near side of Brace's Rock. In the course of painting he further submitted his forms to that familiar ordering of the total design. Strictly repeated horizontals carefully lock the beach, the two points of land, and the horizon line into place. Further, the two fingers of land extending in from the right are complemented by the two protruding masts leaning inward from the left.

Another version, actually dated 1864 (*Ill. 101*), is not quite so successful in a few details. For example, the wrecked hull turns outward rather than inward, which leads the eye away from the central subject. The two points of land are not as cleanly distinguished from each other; the reflections of one overlap too much with the silhouetted rocks of the other. Finally, the foreground flowers are less crisply drawn and colored. But these are minor distinctions. In both pictures, the last rays of pink sunlight stretch across the tip of Brace's Rock, as the distant power of light once more extends intangible fingers across Lane's landscape.

Lane did not visit Maine in 1864, but he remained active and continued to go on drawing expeditions around the Cape Ann Area. With Joseph and Caroline Stevens he made a trip to draw *Eagle Cliff at Old Neck Beach, Manchester,* "one of the sketches made on our last excursion." In July Lane sketched *Folly Cove, Lanesville;* it is fitting that his last dated drawing was in the town named for his ancestors. "Lane and Champney took a drive around the Cape. Champney sketched Folly Cove in colors, Lane in pencil. This was his last excursion in that vicinity. He made no painting from the sketch." Stevens's notation indicates that Lane remained in touch with his old friend Champney, whom he had met and worked with so many years before at Pendleton's in Boston.

In fact, Samuel Sawyer's Diaries and Account Books for these years reveal that artists and works of art were regularly appearing in Gloucester. A frequent patron of Lane and others, Sawyer must have brought some works of art in his collection to Lane's attention. For example, he owned a variety of Italian and Dutch prints and paintings; in 1853 he purchased prints of "Sea Views. Backhuysen." More interesting are Sawyer's notes about the French sculptress Rosa Bonheur. On July 14, 1861, he recorded, "Rosa Bonheur presented me with a large and beautiful Bull Calf, handsomely marked; it came very unexpectedly." The next year he again noted that "Rosa Bonheur called upon a gentleman up in Dogtown about August 1, 1862." In addition, Sawyer had dealings with several other New England artists, including George Loring Brown. In 1863 he noted that the marine watercolorist Fred M. Cozzens was at No. 89 Water Street, and that "J. W. A. Scott, artist Cambridgeport," who was Lane's former colleague, was in town. During the fall of the following year Scott returned for several visits between September and December. The first entry on September 22, 1864, reads, "J. W. A. Scott—artist, Cambridgeport. Wrote to him inviting him to come to Brookbank on Thursday next to spend a few days." Shortly after, "Scott came. . . . Rainy. Scott making sketches." A week later in early October there was "doubtful weather. . . . Scott making sketches from under the hill of the Cove, Wharf, etc. . . . Scott returned this P.M. at 4:40." Finally, in December, Sawyer "went out to call upon J. W. A. Scott, East Cambridge artist. He had many sketches, some of them taken at Gloucester."[2] Thus it would appear that Scott and Lane could compare notes right up to the end of the latter's career.

Meanwhile, Lane's pictures were still being shown regularly at the Boston Athenaeum. The 1864 catalogue records two oils titled *A Foggy Morning* and *Boston Harbor;* in 1865, G. W. Wales lent two paintings by Lane of *Egg Rock, Nahant.* However, a devastating fire, the second in Lane's lifetime, swept the waterfront of Gloucester in 1864:

Among the losses by the recent disastrous fire, perhaps none will be more deeply felt, or are to be more greatly deplored, than many apparently trivial things, of no value save to the owners. Cherished mementoes of childhood or youth, with their pleasant associations; miniatures of beloved friends, gone to the spirit-land; these no money can replace. Our town is also a loser in the destruction of works of local interest. The balance of the edition of Babson's History of Gloucester, was destroyed, and it will probably be long before there is sufficient call for a new edition. The remaining copies of Lane's beautiful view of Gloucester were also consumed. These losses are to be regretted, but it is no use "crying about spilt milk." Let us rather be thankful that we have had these works, and that so many of our citizens have secured them.[3]

On February 22, Sawyer "went to Gloucester to see the effect of the destructive fire and to contribute to those who were left destitute." While the fire did not reach Lane's stone house, he did lose a large number of his lithographs on sale in waterfront shops. About this time, too, he became very ill and remained in poor health through the spring of 1865. By early summer he improved enough to return to work. At least three new pictures were on easels in his studio at the time of his death. One was *Two Ships in Rough Waters,* known only from an "oil copy of last picture on Fitz Hugh Lane's easel at time of Lane's death by Mary B. Mellen" (Cape Ann Historical Association). Two others were of *Ten Pound Island,* both based on a drawing done in 1864 with the comment, "and from this was taken one of the unfinished pictures for Mrs. S. G. Rogers of Roxbury standing on Lane's easel when he died."

In midsummer he had a bad fall, which weakened him considerably. On August 6, he had a severe setback, possibly a heart attack, and remained seriously ill for a week. He died on August 14, 1865. Lane's most generous patron made no comment in his diary; however, both the Gloucester and Boston papers carried extensive and thoughtful commentaries. *The Gloucester Telegraph* printed an announcement on August 16, noting that "his funeral took place yesterday afternoon, from his late residence, the services being conducted by Rev. Mr. Mountford of Boston." [4] A few days later there followed a longer eulogy attributed at the time to William Winter, a native of Gloucester and one of the foremost writers for the *New York Tribune*:

FITZ H. LANE. It is with no ordinary feeling of sorrow that we notice the decease of the distinguished artist, whose recent death deprived this community of a most estimable citizen, and the World of Art of one of its noblest ornaments. It is not the purpose of this brief notice to enlarge upon the finely developed character of the deceased, however grateful that might be; it is enough to say that it was marked by most sterling integrity, joined to great acuteness of intellect.

Mr. Lane in early youth exhibited uncommon proof of capacity, by drawings of wonderful vigor and truthfulness. These were so admirable, under all the circumstances, that they attracted the notice of the best judges. . . . This great promise of early life was fully redeemed in riper age, when, self-taught, he mastered the difficulties of the Art, and took his place in the front rank of Marine Painters in this country. . . .

Mr. Lane was eminently conscientious, never deviating from an accurate copy of nature as presented to his view. His pictures were carefully considered in reference to perspective, and he never sacrificed truth of delineation for picturesque effects. He even carried this faithfulness at times, perhaps, to too great an extent;

but even in such cases the eye was gratified by the exactitude with which individual objects of interest were rendered. His vessels and other marine objects were perfect portraits.

In the industrious, genial, and unpretending life of Mr. Lane we see an illustration most touching to all who knew him, of the great truth that genius is always energetic, cheerful, modest and self-possessed; and that while it does not seek its own, it strives continually and patiently to beautify and enoble whatever comes within its influence.—W.[5]

The Boston papers were no less complimentary:

He has left behind him a name synonymous with all that is excellent in art and lovely in character. No man was more heartily admired in the town where he has resided so many years, and no death can be more lamented.[6]

This notice was followed by a more extensive commentary:

THE LATE F. H. LANE, MARINE ARTIST. The death of this gifted artist may almost be considered a national loss, at least so far as art is concerned. Mr. Lane was undoubtedly the finest marine painter in this country. We have never seen any paintings equal to his in *perfect accuracy* in all the details of marine architecture and thought, and true natural position on the canvas and complete equipment of vessels. . . . It was this faithfulness in the delineation of vessels, that procured him orders from the largest ship owners of New York and Boston, who did not consider their country rooms (and even their parlors sometimes) furnished, without one of Lane's paintings of some favorite clipper.

But Mr. Lane's genius was not limited to the mere painting of ships alone; he was great also in the whole details of the seacoast; the harbor or haven with its many or few vessels, in storm or in calm, at sunset or sunrise; the rock bound coast with its gigantic boulders lashed by the surges of the storm, or gently washed by the still waters of a summer sea; the pebbly shore and smooth sandbeach, with the adjacent cliffs, light-houses and cottage. All of these various scenes were the frequent subjects of his almost magic pencil, and scores of his paintings portraying those sea-shore views will now be valued as they never were before.

It will be long before the rugged shores of Massachusetts Bay produce again such a gifted pencil as his, to illustrate so truthfully the dear scenes he loved so well. His pure and gentle spirit won the respect and esteem of a refined circle of friends, and his kindness of heart and obliging disposition attached him fondly to all. . . .
—W.B.[7]

Thus Fitz Lane of Gloucester was laid to rest. His grave in the Oak Grove cemetery was not far from the house his family once occupied and where he briefly had his studio. He was buried in the Stevens family plot, next to the eventual resting places of Joseph and Caroline. Several bequests in his will are illuminating, as the following excerpts show:

> Fourth: I give to the inhabitants of the town of Gloucester the picture of the old fort, to be kept as a memento of one of the localities of olden time. The said picture now hanging in the reading room under the Gloucester bank, and to be there kept until the town of Gloucester shall furnish a suitable and safe place to hang it.

> Fifth: I give the beautiful wreath of wax flowers (wrought by Mrs. Mary B. Mellen) to Mrs. Caroline Stevens, wife of Joseph L. Stevens, Jr. of said Gloucester.

> Sixth: The picture of my mother, I give to my Brother.

> Seventh: My own portrait, I give to Mrs. Mary B. Mellen of Taunton, state of Massachusetts.[8]

Among a variety of friends he divided a bequest of five hundred dollars, and he appointed Joseph Stevens, Jr., as executor of his estate. In the will are the names of cruising companions, patrons, relatives, and life-long friends. Notably missing are Lane's sister and brother-in-law, the Winters, with whom he had quarreled three years before. Never married, he left personal mementoes, characteristically itemized with care, to those individuals who had sustained him most. Of course, what he left beyond this were serene visions of a better day.

EPILOGUE

Fitz Lane's grave went unmarked for almost a century after his death, until 1960, when E. Hyde Cox, President of the Cape Ann Historical Association, arranged for a stone to be cut and put in place. Ironically, a few years later a drawing by Joseph Stevens was discovered depicting a proposed "stone to memory of Fitz H. Lane of Gloucester, Mass."

Further recognition has come in the recent efforts to save the old stone house and in the mounting of a large retrospective exhibition at the De-Cordova Museum in Lincoln, Massachusetts, in 1966. The only comparable exhibition was held in Gloucester in 1892, when some three hundred pictures by local artists were shown as part of a town anniversary celebration. Of the twenty-two Lanes then on view, almost all have become a part of the permanent collection at the Cape Ann Historical Association. Only one other effort in the twentieth century was made to show Lane's work: A small selection, along with several Heades, was exhibited at M. Knoedler and Co. in New York in 1954. After his lifetime, Lane was largely overlooked, like many of his contemporaries, for several successive generations. This reflected changes in American taste during the second half of the nineteenth century: Homer and Eakins introduced a more heroic type of realism; Whistler and Sargent represented the more fashionable and international tastes that found the generation of the Hudson River School parochial and calculated.

In the early twentieth century the new attention artists devoted to life in the city was at first an effort to capture the feeling and pace of a new age; but in America this eventually led to a renewed pride and interest in the national past. It took two waves of realism—the regionalists of the 1930's and the Pop painters of the 1960's—to revive fully in America an appreciation for its earlier nineteenth-century art. On the hundredth anniversary of Lane's death, the late Charles Olson of Gloucester, one of America's most influential experimental poets, published a commemorative tribute to the Gloucester artist:

An "enthusiasm"

Lane painted true color, and drew
true lines, and 'View' as a prin-
ciple he had also made true as a-
gainst too easy (Dutch) or even a
more brilliant landscape Turner,
Constable (Guardi Canaletto Tie-
polo even behind theirs)
What kept him 'local' or at least provincial
(and patriotic, literally, especially in his
ship scenes, and in fact his introduction of
ships into his scenes, when they weren't there,
and he added them
        was rather a weakness of selection,
        some selecting necessity his principle
        of View called for if his lines and color
        were to be like it first principle
Or some proposal or Vision like in fact Parkman
by making France-American his subject grabbed off.
    It would be impossible to say, and from my own point of view
there wasn't anything at all wrong with 'Gloucester' actually
as such a proposal (And my own experience of his paintings
and his drawings is that with the isolated exception of Castine
the contrast is his
Boston Harbor or Beacon Hill
his New York Harbor and
his Savannah and San Juan Porto Rico paintings
his Gloucesters are altogether his best. It is as though
he got as far as Parkman and Prescott and even as far as
Noah Webster (in the sense of the virtue of his colors and
line and choices of views in Gloucester & Castine—as against
Owls Head Camden Hills
    Blue Hill Somes Bay Northeast Harbor—
as establishing objects as definitions as exact today as they
were then)
        but that say

Hawthorne (born the same year) or Melville but this is larger
and Parkman is the better reference and certainly Whitman's
grab-off is far away and it may seem irrelevant for me to mention it. But the thing is to be sure Lane's specificity &
"place" in exactly the Who's Who in America sense be found
out: he rates (1814-1865) only the company of the men, &
Gloucester & Castine, I have mentioned not his regional &
dull school & museum & Collectors place of "Artist" & Marine
Painter. He was one of the
chief definers of the American 'practice'—the word is
Charles Peirce's for pragmatism—which is still the con-
spicuous difference of American from any other past or any
other present, no matter how much we are now almost the
true international to which all bow and acknowledge.

In honor of 100th
anniversary of the loss,

1965   Charles Olson [9]

Appreciation of Lane has now reached maturity, although there are many
details about his life and art the interested student would still like to know.

The environs of Gloucester, of course, have continued to attract notable
American painters. In the decade that followed Lane's death, both Winslow
Homer and William Morris Hunt came to paint their bright *plein air* views
of the waterfront and harbor activities. In the opening years of the twentieth
century a variety of artists were working there, including Childe Hassam,
John Sloan, and Stuart Davis. Later, in the 1930's, Marsden Hartley recorded
the memorable shapes of Dogtown's ancient glacial rocks, and today nearby
Rockport is the center of renewed artistic activity.

In the context of this activity it is appropriate that Gloucester should have
at last renewed its own awareness of Lane. The efforts on his behalf of a
poet and two successive presidents of the local museum are symptomatic of
a wider re-evaluation of Lane's place in American art—one that sees him as
a truly significant artist of the nineteenth century. Our perspective—that of a
technology-minded era—tends to make us view Lane's age with increased
nostalgia. His landscapes have an unhurried air that we now often wish back.
The glow of that nostalgia, however, should not distort his clear distillation
of the meaning that nature once had in the American imagination.

PLATE V. *Entrance of Somes Sound from Southwest Harbor,* 1852. Oil on canvas, 24 x 36 inches.
Private collection.

PLATE VI. *Salem Harbor,* 1853. Oil on canvas, 26 x 42 inches.
Museum of Fine Arts, Boston; bequest of Maxim Karolik.

ILLUSTRATIONS

1. *The Burning of the Packet Ship "Boston,"* 1830. Watercolor on paper, 19¼ x 27 inches. Cape Ann Historical Association, Gloucester, Mass.

Left
2. Robert Cooke, Lane at Age 31, 1835. Drawing.
American Antiquarian Society, Worcester, Mass.

3. *View of the Old Building at the Corner of Ann Street,* 1835.
Lithograph, 10½ x 13 inches. Boston Athenaeum.

4. *The Salem Mechanick Light Infantry Quick Step,* 1836. Lithograph, 12½ x 9½ inches. Collection Nina Fletcher Little, Brookline, Mass.

5. *View of the Town of Gloucester, Mass.,* 1836. Lithograph, 13 x 19¾ inches. Cape Ann Historical Association, Gloucester, Mass.

6. *The National Lancers with the Reviewing Officers on Boston Common*, 1837. Lithograph, 18 x 22½ inches.
Museum of Fine Arts, Boston.

7. *View of the Great Conflagration, St. John, New Brunswick*, 1838. Colored Lithograph,
21 x 35 inches.
Private collection.

8. *View of Norwich from the West Side of the River,* 1839. Colored lithograph, 11¾ x 16½ inches.
Private collection.

9. *View in Boston Harbour,* late 1830's. Lithograph, 12 x 18½ inches.
Boston Athenaeum.

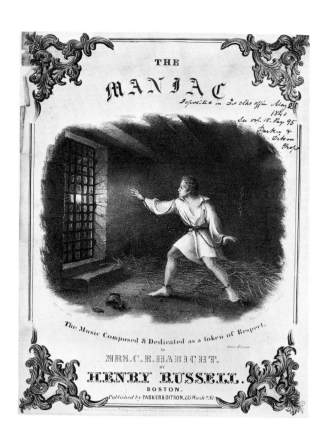

Left

10. *The Maniac*, 1840. Lithographed music sheet cover, 11¼ x 9 inches. Library of Congress.

11. *William H. Harrison, Late President of the United States*, 1841. Lithographed commemorative print, 12 x 9 inches. Library of Congress.

Right
12. *John H. Hawkins,* 1842. Lithograph, 10½ x 9 inches.
Library of Congress.

13. *Alcohol Rocks,* 1842. Lithographed music sheet cover,
10¼ x 8 inches. Library of Congress.

14. *George W. Simmons' Popular Tailoring Establishment, "Oak Hall," Boston, 1844.* Lithographed pamphlet frontispiece, 20¼ x 13¾ inches. Private collection.

Right
15. *Horticultural Hall, c. 1845.* Lithograph, 15 x 10 inches. Boston Athenaeum.

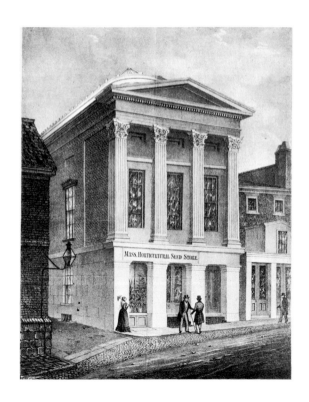

16. *View of Gloucester from Rocky Neck,* 1846. Colored lithograph, 21½ x 35½ inches.
Cape Ann Historical Association, Gloucester, Mass.

17. *Baltimore from Federal Hill,* 1850. Oil on canvas, 18½ x 28 inches.
Shelburne Museum, Shelburne, Vt.

18. *View of Baltimore from Federal Hill,* 1850. Colored lithograph, 18 x 27½ inches. Museum of Fine Arts, Boston, M. and M. Karolik Collection.

19. *View of Gloucester, Mass.,* 1855. Colored lithograph, 21¾ x 35½ inches.
Cape Ann Historical Association, Gloucester, Mass.

20. John W. A. Scott, *Boston Harbor,* 1854. Lithograph, 20 x 30 inches. Boston Athenaeum.

21. *Castine from Hospital Island,* 1855. Colored lithograph, 19¾ x 32¾ inches.
The Mariners Museum, Newport News, Va.

PLATE VII. *Blue Hill, Maine*, mid-1850's. Oil on canvas, 20 x 30 inches. Private collection.

PLATE VIII. *Stage Rocks and Western Shore of Gloucester Outer Harbor*, 1857. Oil on canvas, 23 x 38 inches. Private collection.

PLATE IX. *Riverdale,* 1863. Oil on canvas, 21½ x 35¼ inches.
Cape Ann Historical Association, Gloucester, Mass.; gift of Roger W. Babson.

PLATE X. *Brace's Rock, Eastern Point, Gloucester, c.* 1863. Oil on canvas,
10 x 15 inches. Private collection.

22. *Cunard Liner "Britannia,"* 1842. Oil on canvas, 29¾ x 41¼ inches.
Peabody Museum, Salem, Mass.

23. *Yacht "Northern Light" in Boston Harbor,* 1845. Oil on canvas, 18¾ x 26 inches. Shelburne Museum, Shelburne, Vt.

24. Robert Salmon, *Wharves of Boston,* 1829. Oil on canvas, 40 x 68 inches.
The Bostonian Society, Old State House, Boston.

25. *Boston Harbor, c.* 1847. Oil on panel, 9½ x 13¼ inches.
IBM Corporation, New York.

Below
26. *On the Wharves, Gloucester Harbor,* 1847. Oil on panel, 9¾ x 14½ inches.
Cape Ann Historical Association, Gloucester, Mass.

27. *Gloucester Harbor,* 1848. Oil on canvas, 27¼ x 42 inches.
Virginia Museum of Fine Arts, Richmond, Va.; the Williams Funds, 1962.

28. Lane's Stone House, Duncan's Point, Gloucester, 1850.

Below
29. *View Across Gloucester Inner Cove from Road, near Beach Wharf,* 1850's. Pencil on paper, 9¼ x 22 inches.
Cape Ann Historical Association, Gloucester, Mass.

30. *The Old Fort and Ten Pound Island, Gloucester,* 1850's. Oil on canvas, 22 x 36 inches.
Cape Ann Historical Association, Gloucester, Mass.;
on deposit from the Addison Gilbert Hospital.

31. *The Old Fort and Ten Pound Island, Gloucester,* 1850's. Oil on canvas, 12 x 21¼ inches.
Cape Ann Historical Association, Gloucester, Mass.

32. *St. John's, Porto Rico,* 1850. Oil on canvas, 23¾ x 36¼ inches.
The Mariners Museum, Newport News, Va.

Right
33. *Still Life,* 1849. Oil on panel, 10 x 8¼ inches.
Private collection.

34. *Ten Pound Island at Sunset,* 1851. Oil on panel, 8¼ x 12½ inches. Cape Ann Historical Association, Gloucester, Mass.; gift of Mrs. George Stevens.

35. *Twilight on the Kennebec,* 1849. Oil on canvas, 18 x 30 inches.
Collection Francis Hatch, Castine, Maine.

36. Thomas Cole, *Frenchman Bay, Mount Desert Island,* c. 1845. Oil on canvas, 14 x 23 inches.
Albany Institute of History and Art, Albany, N.Y.

37. Thomas Doughty, *Mount Desert Lighthouse,* 1847. Oil on canvas, 27 x 41 inches.
Newark Museum, Newark, N.J.

38. *Castine from Fort George,* 1850. Oil on canvas, 21 x 33⅜ inches.
Museum of Fine Arts, Boston; M. and M. Karolik Collection.

39. *Bar Island and Mount Desert Mountains from the Bay in Front of Somes Settlement,*
1850. Oil on canvas, 20 x 30 inches.
Private collection.

40. *Off Owl's Head, Maine,* 1852. Oil on canvas, 21 x 36¾ inches.
Cape Ann Historical Association, Gloucester, Mass.

41. *Owl's Head, Penobscot Bay, Maine,* 1862. Oil on canvas, 16 x 26 inches.
Museum of Fine Arts, Boston; M. and M. Karolik Collection.

Below
42. Photograph of Owl's Head from near Monroe Island.

43. *Northeast View of Owl's Head*, 1851. Pencil on paper, 10½ x 16 inches.
Cape Ann Historical Association, Gloucester, Mass.

Below
44. *Castine Harbor and Town*, 1851. Pencil and watercolor on paper, 10¼ x 31¼ inches.
Museum of Fine Arts, Boston; M. and M. Karolik Collection.

45. *Study of Ships,* 1851. Pencil on paper, 6½ x 9 inches. Cape Ann Historical Association, Gloucester, Mass.; gift of Mrs. George Stevens.

Below
46. *Study of Vessels,* 1857. Oil on cardboard, 6¼ x 9½ inches. Cape Ann Historical Association, Gloucester, Mass.; gift of Mrs. George Stevens.

47. *Square-rigged Topsail,* 1850's. Pencil on paper, 7¾ x 11¼ inches. Cape Ann Historical Association, Gloucester, Mass.

Below
48. *Plant and Two Figures,* 1850's. Pen, pencil, and oil on canvas, 6½ x 9¾ inches. Cape Ann Historical Association, Gloucester, Mass.

Above
49. *Seashore Sketch*, 1854. Oil on panel, 6¼ x 9½ inches. Cape Ann Historical Association, Gloucester, Mass.; gift of Mrs. George Stevens.

50. *Steamer "Harvest Moon" Lying at Wharf in Portland*, 1863. Photograph and pencil on paper, 9¾ x 10½ inches. Cape Ann Historical Association, Gloucester, Mass.

51. *Westward View from near East End of Railroad Bridge,* mid-1850's. Pencil on paper,
10 x 16 inches.
Cape Ann Historical Association, Gloucester, Mass.

52. *Looking up Squam River from "Done Fudging,"* mid-1850's. Oil on canvas, 12 x 20
inches.
Cape Ann Historical Association, Gloucester, Mass.

53. *Gloucester from the Outer Harbor,* 1852. Pencil and watercolor on paper, 9½ x 31½
inches.
Cape Ann Historical Association, Gloucester, Mass.

54. *Gloucester Harbor,* 1852. Oil on canvas, 27¼ x 47½ inches.
Cape Ann Historical Association, Gloucester, Mass.;
on deposit from the Town of Gloucester.

55. *Gloucester from Brookbank, c.* 1856. Oil on canvas, 20 x 30 inches.
Museum of Fine Arts, Boston; M. and M. Karolik Collection.

56. *Fresh Water Cove, Gloucester, c.* 1864. Pencil on paper, 10½ x 31¾ inches.
Cape Ann Historical Association, Gloucester, Mass.

57. *Rock Study, c.* 1856. Pencil on paper, 5¼ x 8½ inches. Cape Ann Historical Association, Gloucester, Mass.

Below
58. *Tree Study, c.* 1864. Pencil on paper, 11¼ x 9¼ inches. Cape Ann Historical Association, Gloucester, Mass.

59. *Shipwreck on Stage Rocks, Gloucester*, 1852. Oil on canvas, 27 x 42 inches.
Private collection.

60. *Ships in Ice off Ten Pound Island, Gloucester,* 1850's. Oil on canvas, 12 x 19¾ inches.
Museum of Fine Arts, Boston; M. and M. Karolik Collection.

61. *Half Way Rock*, 1850's. Oil on canvas, 36 x 54 inches.
Collection George Lewis.

62. *Moonlight Fishing Scene (Half Way Rock),* 1854. Oil on canvas, 20 x 28 inches.
Coe Kerr Gallery, Inc., New York.

63. *Camden Hills, Maine,* 1859. Oil on canvas, 20 x 36 inches.
Collection William H. Claflin.

64. *Boston Harbor,* 1853. Oil on canvas, 25¼ x 39¾ inches.
Collection Dr. E. P. Richardson, Jr., Brookline, Mass.

65. *Entrance of Somes Sound from Back of the Island House at Southwest Harbor, Mount Desert*, 1855. Pencil on paper, 16¼ x 16¾ inches. Private collection.

Below
66. *Looking Westerly from Eastern Side of Somes Sound near the Entrance*, 1855. Pencil on paper, 8¾ x 26¼ inches.
Cape Ann Historical Association, Gloucester, Mass.

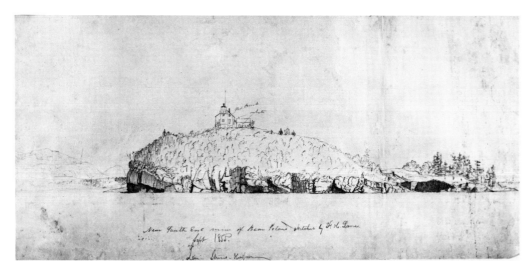

67. *Near Southeast View of Bear Island,* 1855. Pencil on paper, 10¾ x 22¾ inches.
Cape Ann Historical Association, Gloucester, Mass.; gift of Mrs. George Stevens.

Below
68. *Bear Island, Northeast Harbor,* 1855. Oil on canvas, 14 x 21 inches.
Cape Ann Historical Association, Gloucester, Mass.; gift of Mrs. George Stevens.

69. *Off Mount Desert Island, Maine (Entrance of Somes Sound)*, 1850's. Oil on canvas, 20 x 33 inches.
Shelburne Museum, Shelburne, Vt.

70. *Sunrise on the Maine Coast,* 1856. Oil on canvas, 17¼ x 27 inches.
Private collection.

71. *Three Master on the Gloucester Railway,* 1857. Oil on canvas, 39¼ x 59¼ inches.
Cape Ann Historical Association, Gloucester, Mass.;
on deposit from the Town of Gloucester.

72. *Dolliver's Neck and the Western Shore from Field Beach,* 1857. Oil on canvas, 18½ x 32¾ inches.
Cape Ann Historical Association, Gloucester, Mass.

73. *Stage Rocks and Western Shore of Gloucester Outer Harbor,* 1857. Oil on canvas,
15½ x 23½ inches.
Cape Ann Historical Association, Gloucester, Mass.

74. *Stage Fort Rocks,* mid-1850's. Oil on canvas, 13¾ x 24 inches.
Collection Nina Fletcher Little, Brookline, Mass.

75. *Gloucester Harbor at Sunset,* late 1850's. Oil on canvas, 24½ x 38½ inches.
Harvard Business School, Cotting House, Cambridge, Mass.

76. *Boston Harbor at Sunset,* late 1850's. Oil on canvas, 26 x 42 inches.
Museum of Fine Arts, Boston; M. and M. Karolik Collection, by exchange.

77. *Lumber Schooners at Evening on Penobscot Bay,* 1860. Oil on canvas, 28 x 40 inches.
Collection Francis Hatch, Castine, Maine.

78. *Schooners Before Approaching Storm (Off Owl's Head)*, 1860. Oil on canvas, 23½ x
38 inches.
Private collection.

79. *Norman's Woe, Gloucester,* 1862. Oil on canvas, 28 x 50 inches.
Private collection.

80. *The Western Shore with Norman's Woe,* 1862. Oil on canvas, 21½ x 35½ inches.
Cape Ann Historical Association, Gloucester, Mass.

81. Martin Johnson Heade, *Approaching Storm, Beach near Newport, c.* 1867. Oil on canvas, 28 x 58½ inches.
Museum of Fine Arts, Boston; M. and M. Karolik Collection.

82. Mary B. Mellen, *Gloucester Harbor and Dolliver's Neck*, 1870. Oil on canvas, 22¾ x 38 inches.
Collection of Mr. and Mrs. Philip S. Weld, Gloucester, Mass.

83. D. Jerome Elwell, *Gloucester from Dolliver's Neck*, 1880's. Oil on canvas, 16 x 30
inches.
Private collection.

84. John F. Kensett, *Shrewsbury River, New Jersey,* 1859. Oil on canvas, 18½ x 30½ inches.
The New-York Historical Society, New York City.

85. Photograph of Lane late in life, *c.* 1860.
Cape Ann Historical Association, Gloucester, Mass.

Below
86. *"Dream Painting,"* 1862. Oil on canvas, 24 x 36 inches.
Samuel L. Lowe, Jr., Antiques, Inc., Boston.

87. *Christmas Cove, Maine,* 1863. Oil on canvas, 15½ x 24 inches. Private collection.

88. *Indian Bar Cove, Brooksville, Maine,* 1850. Oil on canvas, 11½ x 18¼ inches.
Collection Mr. and Mrs. Joseph H. Davenport, Jr., Lookout Mountain, Tenn.

Below
89. *Moonlight Boating Party (Indian Bar Cove),* 1863. Oil on canvas, 19 x 29 inches.
Private collection.

90. Attributed to Mary B. Mellen, *Moonlight Scene: Gloucester Harbor,* 1870's. Oil on canvas, 13 x 20¼ inches.
Shelburne Museum, Shelburne, Vt.

91. *Lumber Schooner in a Storm,* 1863. Oil on canvas, 23 x 38 inches.
Collection Mr. and Mrs. H. John Heinz, III, Pittsburgh, Pa.

92. Frederic E. Church, *Sunrise off the Maine Coast (Storm off Mount Desert)*, 1863.
Oil on canvas, 37 x 47 inches.
Wadsworth Atheneum, Hartford, Conn.

93. *Ship "Starlight" in the Fog, c.* 1860. Oil on canvas, 30 x 50 inches.
The Butler Institute of American Art, Youngstown, Ohio.

94. William Bradford, *Boston Harbor,* 1857. Oil on canvas, 31½ x 50½ inches. Collection William Bradford Osgood, Boston.

95. Martin Johnson Heade, *Sunrise on the Marshes,* 1863. Oil on canvas, 26¾ x 50¼ inches.
Flint Institute of Arts, Flint, Mich.; gift of the Viola E. Bray Charitable Trust.

96. *Town Parish,* 1863. Pencil on paper, 10½ x 16 inches.
Cape Ann Historical Association, Gloucester, Mass.

Below
97. *Fence with Landscape, c.* 1863. Pencil on paper, 4¼ x 6½ inches.
Cape Ann Historical Association, Gloucester, Mass.

98. *Babson and Ellery Houses, Gloucester,* 1863. Oil on canvas, 21¼ x 35¼ inches. Cape Ann Historical Association, Gloucester, Mass.; gift of Roger W. Babson.

99. Martin Johnson Heade, *The Stranded Boat,* 1863. Oil on canvas, 22¾ x 36½ inches.
Museum of Fine Arts, Boston; M. and M. Karolik Collection.

100. *Brace's Rock, Eastern Point,* 1863. Pencil on paper, 10½ x 15 inches.
Cape Ann Historical Association, Gloucester, Mass.

Below
101. *Brace's Rock, Eastern Point,* 1864. Oil on canvas, 10 x 15 inches.
Collection R. N. Cann, Cambridge, Mass.

APPENDIX

NOTES

BIBLIOGRAPHY

INDEX

APPENDIX
LIST OF LANE'S WORKS
IN PUBLIC COLLECTIONS

OIL PAINTINGS
(in alphabetical order by location)

Addison Gallery of American Art, Andover, Massachusetts
   Fishing Boats at Low Tide, Maine Cove, 1850's. Oil on canvas, 12 x 18 inches.

The Bostonian Society, Old State House, Boston
   Arrival of the Cunard Steamship "Unicorn" in Boston Harbor, Being Greeted by the Revenue Cutter "Hamilton," 1840's. Oil on canvas, 16 x 22 inches.
   Boston Harbor, 1853. Oil on canvas, 32 x 49 inches. Dated: "1853."

Brooklyn Museum, Brooklyn, New York
   Off Mount Desert Island, 1856. Oil on canvas, 23¼ x 36¼ inches. Signed and dated lower left: "F. H. Lane, 1856."

Butler Institute of American Art, Youngstown, Ohio
   Ship "Starlight" in the Fog, c. 1860. Oil on canvas, 30 x 50 inches.

Cape Ann Historical Association, Gloucester, Massachusetts
   Babson and Ellery Houses, Gloucester, 1863. Oil on canvas, 21¼ x 35¼ inches. Signed and dated lower right: "F. H. Lane, 1863." Gift of Roger W. Babson.
   Bear Island, Northeast Harbor, 1855. Oil on canvas, 14 x 21 inches. Gift of Mrs. George Stevens.
   Brig "Cadet" in Gloucester Harbor, late 1840's. Oil on canvas, 15¼ x 23½ inches. Signed lower left: "F. H. Lane."
   A Calm Sea, c. 1860. Oil on canvas, 23¾ x 35½ inches.
   Dolliver's Neck and the Western Shore from Field Beach, 1857. Oil on canvas, 18½ x 32¾ inches
   Gloucester Harbor, 1847. Oil on canvas, 23 x 35½ inches. Signed and dated lower right: "F. H. Lane, 1847."

Gloucester Harbor, 1852. Oil on canvas, 27¼ x 47½ inches. Signed and dated lower right: "Fitz H. Lane, Gloucester, Mass., 1852." On deposit from the Town of Gloucester.

Gloucester Harbor at Sunrise, 1850's. Oil on canvas, 24 x 36 inches. Gift of Lawrence Brooks.

Gloucester Harbor from Rocky Neck, 1844. Oil on canvas, 29½ x 41½ inches. Signed and dated lower right: "F. H. Lane, 1844."

Kettle Island, Manchester, 1859. Oil on canvas, 27 x 46½ inches. Signed and dated lower right: "Fitz H. Lane, 1859."

Looking up Squam River from "Done Fudging," mid-1850's. Oil on canvas, 12 x 20 inches.

Near Owl's Head, Maine, 1850's. Oil on wood, 9 x 11½ inches.

Off Owl's Head, Maine, 1852. Oil on canvas, 21 x 36¾ inches. Signed and dated lower right: "F. H. Lane, 1852."

The Old Fort and Ten Pound Island, Gloucester, 1850's. Oil on canvas, 22 x 36 inches. On deposit from the Addison Gilbert Hospital, Gloucester.

The Old Fort and Ten Pound Island, Gloucester, 1850's. Oil on canvas, 12 x 21¼ inches. Study.

On the Wharves, Gloucester Harbor, 1847. Oil on panel, 9¾ x 14½ inches. Signed and dated on barrel at lower right: "F. H. Lane, 1847."

Riverdale, 1863. Oil on canvas, 21½ x 35¼ inches. Signed and dated lower right: "F. H. Lane, 1863." Gift of Roger W. Babson.

A Rough Sea, c. 1860. Oil on canvas, 23½ x 35½ inches.

Seashore Sketch, 1854. Oil on panel, 6¼ x 9½ inches. On reverse: "F. H. Lane to J. L. Stevens, Jr., 1854." Gift of Mrs. George Stevens.

A Smart Blow, 1856. Oil on canvas, 10 x 15 inches. On reverse: "A Smart Blow by F. H. Lane, 1856."

Somes Sound, Mount Desert Island, Maine, 1850's. Oil on canvas, 10 x 14½ inches.

Stage Rocks and Western Shore of Gloucester Outer Harbor, 1857. Oil on canvas, 15½ x 23½ inches.

Study of Vessels, 1857. Oil on cardboard, 6¼ x 9½ inches. On reverse: "Fitz H. Lane to his friend Joseph L. Stevens, Jr., Gloucester, February 14, 1857." Gift of Mrs. George Stevens.

Ten Pound Island, Gloucester, 1850's. Oil on canvas, 17½ x 29½ inches.

Ten Pound Island at Sunset, 1851. Oil on panel, 8¼ x 12½ inches. On reverse: "Composition, F. H. Lane to J. L. Stevens, Jr. D. Jerome Elwell touched upon, March 13, '91." Gift of Mrs. George Stevens.

Ten Pound Island from Pavilion Beach, 1850's. Oil on canvas, 21½ x 35½ inches. Gift of Isabel B. Lane.

Three Master in Rough Seas, early 1850's. Oil on canvas, 15½ x 23½ inches. Gift of Caroline W. Trask, 1935.

Three Master on the Gloucester Railway, 1857. Oil on canvas, 39¼ x 59¼ inches. On deposit from the Town of Gloucester.

The Western Shore with Norman's Woe, 1862. Oil on canvas, 21½ x 35½ inches.

Chattanooga Art Association, Chattanooga, Tennessee

The "Constitution" in Boston Harbor, c. 1849. Oil on canvas, 14¾ x 22⅛ inches.

Corcoran Gallery of Art, Washington, D.C.

The U. S. Frigate "President" Engaging the British Squadron in 1815, 1851. Oil on canvas, 28 x 42 inches. Signed and dated: "F. H. Lane, 1851." Lansdell K. Christie Collection.

Harvard Business School, Cotting House, Cambridge, Massachusetts

Gloucester Harbor at Sunset, late 1850's. Oil on canvas, 24½ x 38½ inches.

IBM Gallery of Arts and Sciences, New York

Boston Harbor, c. 1847. Oil on panel, 9½ x 13¼ inches. Signed on bow at center: "F. H. Lane."

Marblehead Historical Society, Marblehead, Massachusetts

Surinam Brig in Rough Seas, c. 1850. Oil on panel 9 x 13 inches.

The Mariners' Museum, Newport News, Virginia

Gloucester Inner Harbor, 1850. Oil on canvas, 24 x 36¼ inches. Signed and dated: "F. H. Lane, 1850."

Saint John's Porto Rico, 1850. Oil on canvas, 23¾ x 36¼ inches.

Museum of Art, Rhode Island School of Design, Providence

Little Good Harbor Beach, Cape Ann, 1847. Oil on canvas, 20 x 30 inches. Signed and dated lower left: "F. H. Lane, 1847."

Museum of Fine Arts, Boston

At the Fishing Grounds, 1851. Oil on canvas, 17¼ x 26¼ inches. Signed and dated: "F. H. Lane, 1851." Gift of Caroline W. Trask.

Boston Harbor at Sunset, late 1850's. Oil on canvas, 26 x 42 inches. M. and M. Karolik Collection.

Brig "Antelope" in Boston Harbor, 1863. Oil on canvas, 24¼ x 36 inches. Signed and dated: "F. H. Lane, July, 1863." M. and M. Karolik Collection.

Castine from Fort George, 1850. Oil on canvas, 21 x 33⅜ inches. M. and M. Karolik Collection.

Fresh Water Cove from Dolliver's Neck, 1850's. Oil on canvas, 24 x 36 inches. M. and M. Karolik Collection.

Gloucester from Brookbank, c. 1856. Oil on canvas, 20 x 30 inches. M. and M. Karolik Collection.

Ipswich Bay, 1862. Oil on canvas, 20 x 33 inches. On reverse: "From a sketch made August, 1862." Gift of Mrs. Barclay Tilton.

Moonlight Boating Party (Indian Bar Cove, Brooksville, Maine), 1850. Oil on canvas, 20 x 30 inches. Signed and dated lower right: "F. H. Lane, 1850." Gift of Henry Lee Shattuck.

New York Harbor, 1851. Oil on canvas, 36 x 60 inches. Signed and dated: "Fitz H. Lane, 1851."

Owl's Head, Penobscot Bay, Maine, 1862. Oil on canvas, 16 x 26 inches. On reverse: "Owl's Head, Penobscot Bay, Maine, by F. H. Lane, 1862." M. and M. Karolik Collection.

Salem Harbor, 1853. Oil on canvas, 26 x 42 inches. Signed and dated on sail at center: "F. H. L., 1853." Bequest of Maxim Karolik.

Ships in Ice off Ten Pound Island, Gloucester, 1850's. Oil on canvas, 12 x 19¾ inches. M. and M. Karolik Collection.

Newark Museum, Newark, New Jersey

The Fort and Ten Pound Island, Gloucester, 1848. Oil on canvas, 20 x 30 inches. Signed and dated lower right: "F. H. Lane, 1848."

Peabody Museum, Salem, Massachusetts

Clipper Ship "Southern Cross" in Boston Harbor, 1851. Oil on canvas, 25 x 38 inches. Signed and dated lower right: "F. H. Lane, 1851." Future gift of Stephen Wheatland.

Cunard Liner "Britannia," 1842. Oil on canvas, 29¾ x 41¼ inches. Signed and dated lower right: "F. H. Lane, 1842."

Ship "Samuel Lawrence," 1851. Oil on canvas, 27 x 35¾ inches. Signed and dated: "F. H. Lane, 1851."

The Yacht "America" Winning the International Race, 1851. Oil on canvas, 24¼ x 38¼ inches. Signed and dated: "F. H. Lane, 1851." After a lithograph by Thomas Dutton.

Sargent-Murray-Gilman-Hough House, Gloucester

Stage Fort Across Gloucester Harbor, 1862. Oil on canvas, 38 x 60 inches. Signed and dated lower right: "Fitz H. Lane, 1862."

Watch House Point, 1850's. Oil on canvas, 18 x 23¾ inches. Gift of Mrs. Marie Parsons.

Sawyer Free Library, Gloucester

Gloucester Harbor, 1850's. Oil on canvas, 23¼ x 35¼ inches.

The Sawyer Homestead, c. 1864. Oil on canvas, 23½ x 39½ inches.

Schooner Hauling Granite in Rough Seas, c. 1850. Oil on canvas, 24¾ x 42 inches.

Shelburne Museum, Shelburne, Vermont

Baltimore from Federal Hill, 1850. Oil on canvas, 18½ x 28 inches.

Merchantmen off Boston Harbor, 1862. Oil on canvas, 24¼ x 39¼ inches. Signed and dated: "F. H. Lane, 1862."

New York Yacht Club Regatta, 1857. Oil on canvas, 28 x 48 inches.

Off Mount Desert Island, Maine (Entrance of Somes Sound), 1850's. Oil on canvas, 20 x 33 inches.

Ships Leaving Boston Harbor, 1847. Oil on canvas, 20 x 30 inches. Signed and dated: "F. H. Lane, 1847."

Sunrise Through Mist: Pigeon Cove, Gloucester, 1852. Oil on canvas, 24 x 36 inches. Signed and dated: "F. H. Lane, 1852."

Yacht "Northern Light" in Boston Harbor, 1845. Oil on canvas, 18¾ x 26 inches. On reverse before relining: "After a sketch by Robert Salmon."

Virginia Museum of Fine Arts, Richmond

    Gloucester Harbor, 1848. Oil on canvas, 27¼ x 42 inches. Signed and dated lower right: "F. H. Lane, Jan. 1848."

The White House, Washington, D. C.

    Boston Harbor, 1854. Oil on canvas, 23 x 39 inches. Signed and dated lower right: "F. H. Lane, 1854."

William A. Farnsworth Library and Art Museum, Rockland, Maine

    Penobscot Bay from the Southwest Chamber Window, 1851. Oil on canvas, 11⅛ x 17 inches. On reverse: "Penobscot Bay from the Southwest Chamber Window, F. H. Lane to J. L. Stevens, Jr., 1851."

    Pretty Marsh, Mount Desert Island, c. 1850. Oil on canvas, 10½ x 18 inches.

    Shipping in Down East Waters, 1850's. Oil on canvas, 18 x 30½ inches.

Witherle Memorial Library, Castine, Maine

    Castine from Fort George, 1850. Oil on canvas, 22 x 34 inches.

    Castine Harbor and Town, 1851. Oil on canvas, 20 x 33¼ inches. Signed and dated lower right: "F. H. Lane, 1851."

DRAWINGS AND WATERCOLORS
(in alphabetical order by location)

Cape Ann Historical Association, Gloucester, Massachusetts

    Beach and Pavilion, 1850's. Pencil on paper, 9¼ x 21¾ inches. Signed lower center: "F. H. Lane del."

    Beached Hull, 1862. Pencil on paper, 14 x 15 inches. Signed lower left: "Fitz H. Lane." Sketch for *"Dream Painting."*

    Bear Island from the South, 1855. Pencil on paper, 10½ x 16 inches. Signed and dated top center: "F. H. Lane del., Sept. 1855."

    Bear Island from Western Side of N. East Harbour, 1855. Pencil on paper, 10½ x 21½ inches. Signed and dated lower center: "F. H. Lane del., Sept. 1855."

    Boston Harbor, 1850's. Pencil on paper, 7 x 19½ inches. Signed: "F. H. Lane del."

    Brace's Cove, Eastern Point, 1863. Pencil on paper, 10¾ x 15 inches. Signed and dated lower left: "F. H. Lane, Aug. 1863."

    Brace's Rock, Eastern Point, 1863. Pencil on paper, 10½ x 15 inches. Signed and dated lower center: "F. H. Lane del., Aug. 1863."

    Brig "Agenosa" Laying in Gloucester Harbor—Bound for Surinam, 1852. Pencil and watercolor on paper, 6½ x 9¾ inches. Dated lower left: "Dec. 1852." Signed lower right: "Fitz H. Lane."

    "Bugi's Tape" from Borneo and Celebes, 1850's. Pencil on paper, 9½ x 13¼ inches.

    The Burning of the Packet Ship "Boston," 1830. Watercolor on paper, 19¼ x 27 inches. After a sketch by E. D. Knight.

    Camden Mountains and Harbor from the North Point of Negro Island, 1855. Pencil on paper, 10½ x 25½ inches. Dated: "Sept. 1855."

Camden Mountains from the Penobscot Bay, 1851. Pencil on paper, 10½ x 16 inches. Signed and dated: "F. H. Lane, August 1851."

Camden Mountains from the South Entrance to Harbor, 1855. Pencil on paper, 10½ x 26 inches. Signed and dated: "F. H. Lane del., Sept. 1855."

Camden Mountains from the South West, 1855. Pencil on paper, 10¾ x 25 inches. Signed and dated: "F. H. Lane, del., Sept. 1855."

Camden Mountains from the Waves, 1855. Pencil on paper, 8¾ x 21½ inches. Signed and dated: "F. H. Lane del., Sept. 1855."

Castine from Fort Preble, 1851. Pencil on paper, 10¼ x 27¾ inches. Signed and dated: "F. H. Lane, del., Aug. 1851."

Castine from Heights East of Negro Island, 1855. Pencil on paper, 6¾ x 19¾ inches. Signed and dated: "F. H. Lane del., Sept. 1855."

Castine from Hospital Island, 1855. Pencil on paper, 10 x 52 inches. Signed and dated: "F. H. Lane del., Sept. 1855. Original of my lithograph."

Chebacco River, etc., from West Parish of Gloucester, 1850's. Pencil on paper, 10½ x 24½ inches. Signed: "Sketched by F. H. Lane."

Coffins Beach from the Loaf, 1862. Pencil on paper, 7¼ x 17¼ inches. Signed and dated lower center: "F. H. Lane del., 1862."

Duck Harbor, Isle Au Haut, Penobscot Bay, Me., 1852. Pencil on paper, 10¼ x 31 inches. Signed and dated: "F. H. Lane, Aug. 1852."

Eagle Cliff at Old Neck Beach, Manchester, 1864. Pencil on paper, 10½ x 18½ inches. Signed and dated: "F. H. Lane del., 1864."

Eagle Cliff at Old Neck Beach, Manchester, 1864. Pencil on paper, 10½ x 25½ inches. Signed and dated: "F. H. Lane del., 1864."

Father's [Stevens's] Old Boat, 1851. Pencil on paper, 10¼ x 15¾ inches. Dated: "Aug. 1851."

Fence with Landscape, c. 1863. Pencil on paper, 4¼ x 6½ inches. Signed lower left: "Lane del."

Field Beach and Fresh Water Cove, 1857. Pencil on paper, 9¾ x 23¾ inches. Signed and dated: "F. H. Lane del., 1857."

Folly Cove, Lanesville—Gloucester, 1864. Pencil on paper, 9¼ x 28¼ inches. Signed and dated lower center: "F. H. Lane del., July 1864."

Fremont's Encampment at the Loaf, West Gloucester, 1862. Pencil on paper, 8½ x 20 inches. Signed lower center: "Sketched by F. H. Lane."

Fresh Water Cove, etc., from Dolliver's Neck, 1850's. Pencil on paper, 10½ x 41½ inches. Signed: "F. H. Lane del."

Fresh Water Cove, Gloucester, c. 1864. Pencil on paper, 10½ x 31¾ inches. Signed lower center: "F. H. Lane del."

"General Gates" at Anchor off Our Encampment at Bar Island in Somes Sound, Mount Desert, Maine, 1850. Pencil on paper, 9½ x 11 inches. Signed and dated: "F. H. Lane, Aug. 1850."

Gloucester Beach from the Cut, 1850's. Pencil on paper, 8¾ x 21½ inches. Signed lower center: "F. H. Lane del."

Gloucester from Brookbank, 1856. Pencil on paper, 9½ x 28¼ inches. Signed lower center: "F. H. Lane del."

Gloucester from Fresh Water Cove, 1850's. Pencil on paper, 7 x 28¾ inches. Signed: "F. H. Lane del."

Gloucester from Steepbank, 1850's. Pencil on paper, 10¼ x 16 inches. Signed lower center: "F. H. Lane, del."

Gloucester from the Outer Harbor, 1852. Pencil and watercolor on paper, 9½ x 31½ inches. Signed lower center: "F. H. Lane del."

Gloucester Outer Harbor, from the Cut; and, on reverse, *Across Gloucester Outer Harbor from Steepbank*, 1850's. Pencil on paper, 10½ x 29 inches. Both sides signed: "F. H. Lane del."

Gloucester Outer Harbor from Eastern Point; and, on reverse, *Three Men, One in a Wherry*, 1850's. Pencil on paper, 8½ x 11 inches. Signed: "F. H. Lane del."

Gooloo Pirate's Prow, 1850's. Pencil and paper, 9½ x 14¼ inches.

Little Good Harbor Beach from the Western Upland, 1861. Pencil on paper, 10¼ x 31½ inches. Signed and dated: "F. H. Lane, Wednesday afternoon, Aug. 28, 1861."

Looking Outward from Head of Harbor, 1850's. Pencil on paper, 8¾ x 12¼ inches. Signed: "F. H. Lane del."

Looking up Portland Harbor, 1863. Pencil on paper, 9½ x 29½ inches. Signed and dated: "F. H. Lane del., Aug. 1863."

Looking Westerly from Eastern Side of Somes Sound near the Entrance, 1855. Pencil on paper, 8¾ x 26¼ inches. Signed and dated upper right: "by F. H. Lane, September, 1855."

Majebigweduer Narrows from North Castine, 1850. Pencil on paper, 9½ x 18 inches. Signed and dated: "F. H. Lane del., Aug. 1850."

Manchester, Bakers Island, from West Manchester Shore, 1850's. Pencil on paper, 9¼ x 14 inches. Signed: "F. H. Lane."

Mount Desert Mountains, from Bar Island, Somes Sound, 1850. Pencil on paper, 8 x 21½ inches. Signed and dated: "F. H. Lane del., Aug. 1850."

Mount Desert Sketch, 1850's. Pencil on paper, 9½ x 20½ inches. Signed: "F. H. Lane."

Music sheet design, 1840's. Pen on paper, 5 x 7½ inches. Signed: "Fitz H. Lane." (Pasted into *Album of Gloucester Artists*.)

Near Southeast View of Bear Island, 1855. Pencil on paper, 10¾ x 22¾ inches. Signed and dated lower center: "Sketched by F. H. Lane, Sept. 1855." Gift of Mrs. George Stevens.

Near West Beach, Beverly, 1850's. Pencil on paper, 10½ x 29 inches. Signed: "F. H. Lane del."

Norman's Woe, 1861. Pencil on paper, 8½ x 25½ inches. Signed and dated lower center: "F. H. Lane del., 1861."

North East Harbor, Mount Desert, 1850. Pencil on paper, 9½ x 20¾ inches. Signed and dated: "F. H. Lane, Aug. 1850."

North View of Owl's Head, 1855. Pencil on paper, 10¼ x 16 inches. Signed and dated: "F. H. Lane del., Sept. 1855."

North Westerly View of Mount Desert Rock, 1852. Pencil on paper, 10¼ x 16 inches. Signed and dated lower right: "F. H. Lane del., Aug. 1852."

Northeast view of Owl's Head, 1851. Pencil on paper, 10½ x 16 inches. Signed and dated lower center: "Aug. 1851, by F. H. Lane."

Old Neck Beach at Manchester, 1864. Pencil on paper, 10½ x 25¼ inches. Signed and dated: "F. H. Lane del., 1864."

Owl's Head from the South, 1851. Pencil on paper, 10¼ x 15¾ inches. Signed and dated: "F. H. Lane, Aug. 1851."

Pavilion, 1850's. Pencil on paper, 10½ x 16¼ inches. Signed: "F. H. Lane del."

Plant and Two Figures, 1850's. Pen, pencil, and oil on canvas, 6½ x 9¾ inches. Signed three times: "Lane del."

Rock Study, c. 1856. Pencil on paper, 5¼ x 8½ inches. Signed lower center: "Lane del."

Rocks, 1850's. Pencil on paper, 7¼ x 9½ inches. Signed: "Lane del."

Shoreline with Sloop and Wharf in Foreground, 1850's. Pencil on paper, 10½ x 28¾ inches. Signed: "F. H. Lane del."

Sketch from Gloucester Outer Harbor, 1863. Pencil on paper, 10½ x 43½ inches. Signed and dated: "F. H. Lane, 1863."

Sloop, early 1850's. Pencil on paper, 9½ x 11¾ inches. Signed: "Lane del."

Sloop "Superior"; and, on reverse, Two Men in Rowboat, early 1850's. Pencil on paper, 13¾ x 10¼ inches.

Sloop with Study of Masthead Rigging, 1850's. Pencil on paper, 10¾ x 14¼ inches. Signed: "Lane del."

Somes Sound, Looking Southerly, 1850. Pencil on paper, 9½ x 19¾ inches. Signed and dated lower center: "F. H. Lane, August 1850."

South East View of Owl's Head, from the Island, 1855. Pencil on paper, 10¾ x 25½ inches. Signed and dated: "F. H. Lane del., Sept. 1855."

South East View of Owl's Head, from the Point of the Island, 1855. Pencil on paper, 10½ x 30½ inches. Signed and dated: "F. H. Lane, Sept. 1855."

South View of Owl's Head, from the S. End of the Island, 1855. Pencil on paper, 8¼ x 28 inches. Signed and dated: "F. H. Lane, Sept. 1855."

Southwest Harbor, Mount Desert, 1852. Pencil on paper, 10½ x 31¾ inches. Signed and dated: "F. H. Lane, Aug. 1852."

Square-rigged Topsail, 1850's. Pencil on paper, 7¾ x 11¼ inches. Signed: "Lane del."

Stage Rocks and Western Shore of Gloucester Outer Harbor, 1857. Pencil on paper, 10½ x 32¼ inches. Signed: "F. H. Lane."

Steamer "Harvest Moon," Lying at Wharf in Portland, 1863. Photograph and pencil on paper, 9¾ x 10½ inches. Signed and dated lower left: "by Lane, 1863."

Study of Ships, 1851. Pencil on paper, 6½ x 9 inches. Signed and dated lower right: "Fitz H. Lane, 1851." Gift of Mrs. George Stevens.

Supposed "Oldest House in Town," and *Parson White Town Parish, c.* 1860. Pencil on paper, 11¼ x 16¼ inches.

Ten Pound Island in Gloucester Harbor, 1850's. Pencil on paper, 9 x 11¼ inches. Signed: "F. H. Lane del."

Ten Pound Island in Gloucester Harbor, 1864. Pencil on paper, 10½ x 15 inches. Signed and dated: "F. H. Lane del., 1864."

Three Cows and Temple, 1850's. Pen and pencil on paper, 10¼ x 11¾ inches.

Three Master, 1850's. Pencil on paper, 6 x 13 inches.

Three Master at Sea, 1850's. Pencil on paper, 6 x 8¾ inches.

Tow Boat, 1850's. Pencil on paper, 8¼ x 11 inches. Signed lower right: "F. H. Lane del."

Town Parish, 1863. Pencil on paper, 10½ x 16 inches. Signed lower center: "F. H. Lane del."

Tree Study; and, on reverse, *Manchester Beach, c.* 1864. Pencil on paper, 11¼ x 9¼ inches. Signed on both sides: "F. H. Lane del."

Two Oxen, 1850's. Pencil on paper, 8 x 9¼ inches. Signed: "Lane del."

Two Vessels, 1850's. Pencil on paper, 7¾ x 11 inches. Signed: "Lane del."

View Across Gloucester Inner Cove, from Road near Beach Wharf, 1850's. Pencil on paper, 9¼ x 22 inches. Signed: "F. H. Lane del."

View Across the Marsh and Mill Pond in Town Parish, 1863. Pencil on paper, 10 x 26 inches. Signed lower center: "F. H. Lane, del."

View at Bass Rocks Looking Eastward, 1850's. Pencil on paper, 10¼ x 43½ inches. Signed: "F. H. Lane del."

View at West Beach, Beverly, 1850's. Pencil on paper, 10½ x 34 inches. Signed: "F. H. Lane del."

View from Rocky Neck, Gloucester, 1850's. Pencil on paper, 9 x 34 inches. Signed: "F. H. Lane del."

View from Stage Rocks, Gloucester, 1850's. Pencil on paper, 10 x 36 inches.

View in Gloucester Harbor, 1850's. Pencil on paper, 9¼ x 32¾ inches. Signed: "F. H. Lane del."

View in Town Parish, 1863. Pencil on paper, 9¾ x 29 inches. Signed lower center: "F. H. Lane del."

View in West Parish on Lower Road, c. 1863. Pencil on paper, 9¼ x 27¼ inches. Signed: "F. H. Lane del."

View of Bar Island and Mount Desert Mountains, from the Bay in Front of Somes Settlement, 1850. Pencil on paper, 9 x 20 inches. Signed upper left: "Lane del." Dated lower right: "Aug. 1850."

West Harbor and Entrance to Somes Sound, 1852. Pencil on paper, 10½ x 16 inches. Signed and dated: "F. H. Lane del., Aug. 1852."

Western Shore of Gloucester Outer Harbor, 1857. Pencil on paper, 9 x 28 inches. Signed lower center: "F. H. Lane del."

Western View of High Head Neck, 1850. Pencil on paper, 9½ x 23¾ inches. Signed and dated: "F. H. Lane del., Aug. 1850."

Westward View from House near "Done Fudging," 1861. Pencil on paper, 6¾ x 15 inches. Signed and dated: "F. H. Lane del., Thursday, Aug. 29, 1861."

Westward View from near East End of Railroad Bridge, mid-1850's. Pencil on paper, 10 x 16 inches. Signed: "F. H. Lane del."

Museum of Fine Arts, Boston

Castine Harbor and Town, 1851. Pencil and watercolor on paper, 10¼ x 31¼ inches. Signed and dated: "F. H. Lane del. August, 1851."

William A. Farnsworth Library and Art Museum, Rockland, Maine

Castine from Fort George, 1850. Pencil on paper, 9 x 31¼ inches.

LITHOGRAPHS AND ENGRAVINGS
(in alphabetical order by title)

NOTE: *Since in most cases multiple copies are known for these prints, locations are not given. The largest public collection of Lane lithographs are in the American Antiquarian Association, Worcester, Massachusetts; The Boston Athenaeum; The Library of Congress, Washington, D.C.; The Mariners' Museum, Newport News, Virginia; and The New York Public Library.*

Alcohol Rocks, 1842. Lithographed music sheet cover, 10¼ x 8 inches. Published by E. W. Bouvé.

Ariel Waltz, c. 1840. Lithographed music sheet cover, 15 x 11 inches.

Auxiliary Steam Packet Ship "Massachusetts," 1845. Lithograph, 14½ x 20 inches. "F. H. Lane, del." Lane & Scott's Lithography, Boston.

Boston, March 28th, 1847, Departure of the "Jamestown" for Cork, Ireland, E. B. Forbes, Commander, 1847. Lithograph, 4½ x 7¾ inches. "On Shore by F. H. Lane." Lane and Scott's Lithography, Boston.

Bowdoin College, Brunswick, Me., mid-1840's. Lithograph, 6 x 11½ inches. Lane and Scott's Lithography, Boston. Published by J. Griffin.

Burbanville to Blackstone River, late 1830's. Lithographed music sheet cover, 16 x 10½ inches. Moore's Lithography, Boston.

Byron's Dungeon, c. 1840. Lithographed music sheet cover, 10 x 8 inches.

Captn. E. G. Austin's Quick Step, 1837. Lithographed music sheet cover, 13 x 10 inches. Published by Parker & Disson, Boston.

Castine from Hospital Island, 1855. Colored lithograph, 19¾ x 32¾ inches. Published by Joseph L. Stevens, Jr. L. H. Bradford's Lithography, Boston.

Commercial Coffee House, c. 1846. Lithographed advertisement, 9 x 13 inches. Lane and Scott's Lithography, Boston.

First Parish Meeting House, 1738–1826, 1860. Lithographed illustration, 4 x 6¾ inches. J. J. Babson, *History of Gloucester,* app. 498.

Fore-and-Aft Sail on Mizzen Mast, 1860. Wood engraved illustration, 2¼ x 2¼ inches. J. J. Babson, *History of Gloucester,* 254.

The Fulton Iron Foundry, c. 1842. Lithographed advertisement, 12 x 10 inches. "F. H. Lane del." J. C. Sharp's Lithography, Boston.

George W. Simmons' Popular Tailoring Establishment, "Oak Hall," Boston, 1844. Lithographed pamphlet frontispiece, 20¼ x 13¾ inches. "F. H. Lane del." Lane and Scott's Lithography, Boston.

Horticultural Hall, c. 1845. Lithograph, 15 x 10 inches. Lane and Scott's Lithography, Boston.

John H. W. Hawkins, 1842. Lithograph, 10½ x 9 inches. "On stone by F. H. Lane." After a drawing by T. M. Burnham. J. C. Sharp's Lithography, Boston.

Lawrence Quick Step, 1839. Lithographed music sheet cover, 15 x 11 inches. "Drawn by F. H. Lane." Published by Charles Keith, Boston.

Love Among The Roses, c. 1840. Lithographed music sheet cover, 11 x 9 inches. Pendleton's Lithography, Boston.

The Mad Girl's Song, 1840. Lithographed music sheet cover, 12 x 9 inches. "F. H. Lane del." Thayer's Lithography, Boston. Published by Oakes & Swan, Boston.

The Maniac, 1840. Lithographed music sheet cover, 11¼ x 9 inches. "On stone by F. H. Lane." Thayer's Lithography, Boston.

Mariner Loves O'er the Waters to Roam, 1840. Lithographed music sheet cover, 11 x 9 inches.

Mariner's Return, 1841. Lithographed music sheet cover, 11 x 9 inches. Published by George P. Reed, Boston.

Millbury Village, late 1830's. Lithograph, 10½ x 16 inches. "Drawn by F. H. Lane." Moore's Lithography, Boston.

The Nahant Quadrilles, 1836. Lithographed music sheet cover, 15 x 11 inches. "F. H. Lane del." Moore's Lithography, Boston. Published by John F. Nunns, Philadelphia.

The National Lancers with the Reviewing Officers on Boston Common, 1837. Lithograph, 18 x 22½ inches. "On Stone by F. H. Lane." After a drawing by Charles Hubbard. Published by Thomas Moore, Boston.

The New England Guards, 1839. Lithographed certificate, 15 x 11 inches. "Drawn by F. H. Lane." Moore's Lithography, Boston.

Norfolk Guards Quick Step, 1840. Lithographed music sheet cover, 13½ x 8¾ inches. "F. H. Lane del." Published by Oakes and Swan, Boston.

The Old Arm Chair, 1840. Lithographed music sheet cover, 12 x 9 inches. "F. H. Lane del." Thayer's Lithography, Boston. Published by Oakes & Swan, Boston.

Oldest House in Gloucester, 1860. Wood engraved illustration, 2¼ x 3½ inches. J. J. Babson, *History of Gloucester,* 452.

On Ellen's Bloom Blushed a Rose, 1840. Lithographed music sheet cover, 12 x 9 inches. "F. H. Lane del." Thayer's Lithography, Boston. Published by Oakes & Swan, Boston.

Pesky Sarpent, c. 1840. Lithographed music sheet cover, 11 x 9 inches.

The Salem Mechanick Light Infantry Quick Step, 1836. Lithographed music sheet cover, 12½ x 9½ inches. Lower left: "F. H. Lane del." Moore's Lithography, Boston (successor to Pendleton). Published by Ives & Putnam, Salem, Mass.

Second Parish Meeting House, 1860. Wood engraved illustration, 2¼ x 3½ inches. J. J. Babson, *History of Gloucester,* 266.

Ship Dismasted at Sea, 1890's. Lithograph, 11 x 15 inches.

Song of the Fisher's Wife, 1840. Lithographed music sheet cover, 12 x 9 inches. "F. H. Lane del." Sharp & Michelin, Printers. Published by Oakes & Swan, Boston.

Steam Demi Bark "Antelope," 615 Tons, 1855. Lithographed illustration, 8¼ x 14¼ inches. "From a painting by F. H. Lane." J. H. Bufford's Lithography, Boston. Lithographed expressly for the *Nautical Magazine.*

Steam Packet Ship "Massachusetts" in a Squall, Nov. 10, 1845, 1845. Lithograph, 15¼ x 21¾ inches. "F. H. Lane del." Lane & Scott's Lithography, Boston.

View in Boston Harbour, late 1830's. Lithograph, 12 x 18½ inches. "Drawn on stone by F. H. Lane." Thomas Moore's Lithography, Boston. "Respectfully dedicated to the Tiger Boat Club by their obt. serv't. Th. Moore."

View of Baltimore from Federal Hill, 1850. Colored lithograph, 18 x 27½ inches. "Sketched from nature by F. H. Lane." Saroney & Major Lithographers, N.Y. Published by A. Conant.

View of Gloucester from Rocky Neck, 1846. Colored lithograph, 21½ x 35½ inches. "Drawn by F. H. Lane." Lane and Scott's Lithography, Boston.

View of Gloucester, Mass., 1855. Colored lithograph, 21¾ x 35½ inches. Bradford's Lithography, Boston.

View of Gloucester, Mass., from Ten Pound Island, 1851. Colored lithography, 13 x 20 inches. M. M. Tidd's Lithography, Boston.

View of Lowell, Mass., late 1830's. Lithography, 9 x 15¾ inches. Moore's Lithography, Boston. Published by E. A. Rice & Co., Lowell.

View of New Bedford, from The Fort near Fairhaven, c. 1846. Colored lithograph, 16¼ x 25¼ inches. "F. H. Lane del." From a sketch by A. Conant. Lane & Scott's Lithography, Boston. Published by A. Conant.

View of Newburyport, from Salisbury, 1846. Colored lithograph, 21 x 35 inches. "Drawn on stone by F. H. Lane." After a sketch by A. Conant. Lane and Scott's Lithography, Boston.

A View of Newton Corner, as seen from Fiske Hill, c. 1845. Colored lithograph, 9 x 14½ inches. From a sketch by A. Conant. Lane & Scott's Lithography, Boston.

View of Norwich from the West Side of the River, 1839. Colored lithograph, 11¾ x 16½ inches. Sarony & Major Lithography, New York.

View of the Old Building at the Corner of Ann Street, Boston, 1835. Lithograph, 10½ x 13 inches. Pendleton's Lithography, Boston.

View of Old Fort and Harbor, 1860. Lithographed illustration, 4 x 6¾ inches. J. J. Babson, *History of Gloucester*, opp. 474.

View of the Battle Ground at Concord, Mass., 1856. Colored lithograph, 13 x 19¾ inches. "F. H. Lane del." Thayer's Lithography, Boston.

View of the City of Washington, 1838. Lithograph, 21 x 38 inches. "On stone by F. H. Lane." Moore's Lithography, Boston.

View of the Great Conflagration, St. John, New Brunswick, 1838. Colored lithograph, 21 x 35 inches. "F. H. Lane del." Moore's Lithography, Boston.

View of the Great Western and New York Depot at South Cove, Boston, late 1830's. Lithographed trade card, 6½ x 12 inches. R. Cook's Lithography, Boston.

View of the Town of Gloucester, Mass., 1836. Lithograph, 13 x 19¾ inches. Lower left: "Drawn from nature and on stone by F. H. Lane." Pendleton's Lithography, Boston.

The White-Ellery House, 1860. Wood engraved illustration, 2¼ x 3½ inches. J. J. Babson, *History of Gloucester*, 230.

William H. Harrison, Late President of the United States, 1841. Lithographed commemorative print, 12 x 9 inches. "On stone by F. H. Lane." Thayer's Lithography, Boston.

William H. Ladd's Eating House, late 1830's. Lithographed trade card, 7 x 9½ inches. J. C. Sharp's Lithography, Boston.

Worcester House, c. 1840. Lithograph, 18¾ x 23¾ inches. "F. H. Lane del." Moore's Lithography, Boston.

NOTES

CHAPTER 1

1. Information from *Vital Statistics* of Gloucester; John J. Babson, *History of Gloucester, Cape Ann, Including the Town of Rockport* (Gloucester, 1860), *passim;* and Edward H. Lane, "Early Recollections of Fitz H. Lane," *Gloucester Daily Times,* March 23, 1946.

2. Edward Lane, "Early Recollections."

3. Babson, *History of Gloucester,* p. 258.

4. Edward Lane, "Early Recollections."

5. Susan Babson, "C.A.S. & L.A. Weekly Column on Matters of Local History," *Authors and Artists of Cape Ann* (album of miscellaneous clippings), Cape Ann Historical Association, Gloucester.

6. J. Babson, *History of Gloucester,* p. 258.

7. Letter in Cape Ann Historical Association.

8. See Barbara Novak's discussion of this work in *American Painting of the Nineteenth Century* (New York, 1969), p. 111; also Alfred Mansfield Brooks, "The Packet Ship *Boston* of Gloucester," Essex Institute *Historical Collections* 79 (April, 1943): 114–16.

9. Edward Lane, "Early Recollections."

10. Benjamin Champney, *Sixty Years' Memories of Art and Artists* (Woburn, Mass., 1900), p. 10.

11. Helen Mansfield and John Trask in *Authors and Artists of Cape Ann;* also J. Babson, *History of Gloucester,* p. 258. I am especially grateful to David Tatham of Syracuse University, who brought the Cooke drawing of Lane to my attention.

12. *Gloucester Telegraph,* August 15, 1835.

13. *Ibid.,* December 19, 1835.

14. *Ibid.,* March 16, 1836.

15. Fred W. Tibbetts, "Fitz H. Lane," in "C.A.S. & L.A. Weekly Column on Matters of Local History," *Authors and Artists of Cape Ann.*

CHAPTER 2

1. See Appendix under "Lithographs and Engravings." My thanks to David Tatham for providing me with some titles I had not previously recorded. Large collections of Lane's lithographs are in the Boston Athenaeum, the Mariners' Museum, Newport News, Virginia, and the Library of Congress.

2. Champney, *Sixty Years' Memories,* p. 14.

3. See advertisements for Oak Hall in the Boston *Daily Evening Transcript,* January 5, 1847.

4. *Gloucester Telegraph,* November 25, 1846.

5. J. Babson, *History of Gloucester,* pp. 230, 254, 266, 452, 474, and 498.

CHAPTER 3

1. Boston *Daily Advertiser and Patriot,* July, 4, 1845.

2. See John Wilmerding, *Robert Salmon, Painter of Ship and Shore* (Boston and Salem, 1971).

3. See John Wilmerding, *History of American Marine Painting* (Boston and Toronto, 1968), chaps. VII, VIII, and X.

4. On the *Northern Light,* see the Boston *Daily Evening Transcript,* May 27, 1850. Also see Wilmerding, *Robert Salmon,* chap. 5.

5. Champney, *Sixty Years' Memories,* p. 12.

6. See Wilmerding, *Robert Salmon,* Appendix B.

7. Another painting, *Boston Harbor with Constitution Wharf* (Collection Nina Fletcher Little, Brookline, Mass.), is of comparable scale and design. Also belonging to this group is a larger oil, *Ships Leaving Boston Harbor* (Shelburne Museum, Shelburne, Vt.).

8. Fragment of a newspaper clipping of 1892 in *Authors and Artists of Cape Ann.*

9. J. Babson, *History of Gloucester,* p. 258.

10. *Authors and Artists of Cape Ann.*

11. Edward Lane, "Early Recollections."

12. Boston *Daily Evening Transcript,* May 22, 1850.

13. *Authors and Artists of Cape Ann.*

14. *Ibid.*

15. Champney, *Sixty Years' Memories,* p. 99.

16. *Authors and Artists of Cape Ann.*

CHAPTER 4

1. Instrument of Agreement in Cape Ann Historical Association, dated and signed by Lane November 16, 1849.

2. *Authors and Artists of Cape Ann;* also A. M. Brooks, "The Fitz Lane House in Gloucester," Essex Institute *Historical Collections* 78 (July, 1942): 281.

3. *Authors and Artists of Cape Ann.*

4. *Ibid.*

5. *Ibid.*

6. *Ibid.*

7. Information from files at Frick Art Reference Library, New York.

8. *Authors and Artists of Cape Ann.*

9. *Ibid.*

10. Boston *Daily Evening Transcript,* May 3, 1850.

11. *Ibid.,* Editorial Correspondence, May 10, 1850.

12. See Wilmerding, *History of American Marine Painting,* chap. XII.

13. Quoted in the *Gloucester Telegraph,* November 5, 1851.

14. Boston *Daily Evening Transcript,* February 4, 1851.

CHAPTER 5

1. Mary B. Cowdrey and Theodore Sizer, *American Academy of Fine Arts and American Art-Union Exhibition Record 1816–1852* (New York, 1953), p. 221.

2. See Novak, *American Painting of Nineteenth Century,* chap. 6, *passim,* and notes, 301–2.

3. See Theodore Stebbins, *Martin Johnson Heade* (exhibition catalogue), Whitney Museum, *et al.* (New York, 1969), where he discusses this point. Basing his argument on E. P. Richardson, *Painting in America* (New York, 1956), p. 219, Stebbins suggests the new pigments were not introduced until the late 1850's, and that Church's *Twilight in the Wilderness* was the first major work to employ them. Yet Lane's use of the new colors in 1848 and frequently throughout the whole decade of the 1850's must indicate an earlier date for their availability. It is true that Church's painting was the summary work of this type, and its influence greatly popularized the techniques.

4. Frederic Alan Sharf, "Fitz Hugh Lane: Visits to the Maine Coast, 1848–1855," Essex Institute *Historical Collections* 98 (April, 1962): 115.

5. David C. Huntington, *The Landscapes of Frederic Edwin Church* (New York, 1966), *passim.*

6. Theodore Stebbins *et al., Luminous Landscape, The American Study of Light, 1860–1875* (Exhibition catalogue), Fogg Art Museum (Cambridge, Mass., 1966), pp. 6–7.

7. Sharf, "Visits to the Maine Coast," p. 112.

8. Susan Babson in *Authors and Artists of Cape Ann.*

9. Letter in Cape Ann Historical Association.

10. Sharf, "Visits to the Maine Coast," *loc. cit.*

11. *Ibid.*

12. J. L. Stevens, Jr., in the *Gloucester Daily Telegraph,* September 11, 1850. One painting usually thought to be by Lane from this period is *A Maine Inlet* in the Boston Museum of Fine Arts. It was most recently reproduced as such in James Thomas Flexner's *Nineteenth Century American Painting* (New York, 1970), pp. 76–77. Unfortunately, the painting is almost surely not by Lane. See my "As under a Bell Jar: A Study of Quality in Fitz Hugh Lane," *Antiques* 82 (October, 1962): 406–9.

13. Unless otherwise indicated, all further drawings mentioned are in the Cape Ann Historical Association.

CHAPTER 6

1. Both letters in the Cape Ann Historical Association.

2. Gene McCormick, "Fitz Hugh Lane, Gloucester Artist, 1804–1865," *Art Quarterly* 15 (1852): 288–301; and Barbara Novak, *American Painting of Nineteenth Century,* chap. 6, especially pp. 118–19.

3. *Authors and Artists of Cape Ann.*

4. Cape Ann Historical Association.

5. *Ibid.*

6. Champney, *Sixty Years' Memories,* p. 14.

CHAPTER 7

1. Letter in Cape Ann Historical Association.

2. Sharf, "Visits to the Maine Coast," p. 117.

3. Denis O'Neill has made a probing (if somewhat bombastic) study of the possible Dutch influences in Lane's work, as well as that in such others as Heade, Quidor, and Bingham. Unpublished paper in Carpenter Art Library, Dartmouth College, Hanover, New Hampshire.

4. *Authors and Artists of Cape Ann.*

5. Sharf, "Visits to the Maine Coast," p. 118.

6. *Authors and Artists of Cape Ann.*

7. *Cape Ann Advertiser,* August 1, 1857.

8. *Authors and Artists of Cape Ann.*

9. Fragment of letter in Cape Ann Historical Association.

10. *Ibid.*

11. This idea is closely related to the discussions of luminism by John Baur, Barbara Novak, Theodore Stebbins, and others. This phenomenon in American painting is peculiar to the middle decades of the nineteenth century, and examples can be cited in the work of almost every major painter during that period. See my *Pittura americana dell 'Ottocento* (Milan, 1969). Sylvan Schendler also deals with the idea in the work of Thomas Eakins in his *Eakins* (Boston and Toronto, 1968).

12. Fred W. Tibbetts in *Authors and Artists of Cape Ann.*

CHAPTER 8

1. See Wilmerding, *History of American Marine Painting,* chap. X and XI, where the relationship between Lane and Bradford is discussed at length; and *idem, William Bradford, Painter and Photographer of the Arctic* (Exhibition catalogue), DeCordova Museum (Lincoln, Mass., 1969).

2. Fred W. Tibbetts in *Authors and Artists of Cape Ann.*

3. *Ibid.*

4. *Ibid.*

5. See Wilmerding, *History of American Marine Painting.*

6. Copy of the letter in Stevens's hand in Cape Ann Historical Association. Original owned by Samuel L. Lowe, Jr., Antiques, Inc., Boston.

7. See Wilmerding, *Fitz Hugh Lane, American Marine Painter* (Salem, 1964), where I reproduced it as a Lane and at that time believed it to be one.

CHAPTER 9 AND EPILOGUE

1. Joseph E. Garland, historian of Eastern Point, Gloucester, in correspondence.

2. Sawyer account books and diaries in Cape Ann Historical Association.

3. *Authors and Artists of Cape Ann.*

4. *Gloucester Telegraph,* August 16, 1865.

5. *Ibid.,* August 19, 1865.

6. Boston *Daily Evening Transcript,* August 16, 1865.

7. *Ibid.,* August 19, 1865.

8. Essex Probate Court, Salem, Mass., No. 44900, dated March 17, 1865, proved October 1, 1865. Record Book No. 124, p. 34.

9. *Gloucester Daily Times,* October 9, 1965.

BIBLIOGRAPHY

Authors and Artists of Cape Ann. Unpaged notebook of newspaper and other clippings, plus miscellaneous information, in the Cape Ann Historical Association, Gloucester.

BABSON, JOHN J. *History of Gloucester, Cape Ann, Including the Town of Rockport.* Gloucester, Mass., 1860.

———. *Notes and Additions to the History of Gloucester.* 2 vols. I, Gloucester, Mass., 1876; II, Salem, Mass., 1891 (bound in one volume).

BAUR, JOHN I. H. "Early Studies in Light and Air by American Landscape Painters," *Bulletin,* the Brooklyn Museum 9 (Winter, 1948): 1–9.

———. "Unknown American Painters of the 19th Century," *College Art Journal* 6 (Summer, 1947): 277–82.

BROOKS, ALFRED MANSFIELD. "The Burning of the Packet Ship *Boston,*" Essex Institute *Historical Collections* 79 (April, 1943): 114–16.

———. "The Fitz Hugh Lane House in Gloucester," Essex Institute *Historical Collections* 78 (July, 1942): 281–83.

———. "Fitz Lane's Drawings," Essex Institute *Historical Collections* 81 (January, 1945): 83–86.

CAREY, JOHN THOMAS. "The American Lithograph from its Inception to 1865, with Biographical Consideration of Twenty Lithographers and a Check List of Their Works." Doctoral dissertation, Ohio State University, 1954.

CHAMPNEY, BENJAMIN. *Sixty Years' Memories of Art and Artists.* Woburn, Mass., 1900.

CHILDS, CHARLES D. "Marine Painting: Flood Tide," *Antiques* 66 (July, 1954): 54–55.

Commemorative Exhibition. Paintings by Martin J. Heade and Fitz Hugh Lane from the Karolik Collections in the Museum of Fine Arts, Boston, at M. Knoedler and Co., May, 1954. Introduction by JOHN I. H. BAUR.

HERSCH, PHILIP F. "F. H. Lane: With a Fetish for Red," *Gloucester Daily Times,* July 14, 1967.

HOWAT, JOHN K., and JOHN WILMERDING. *19th-Century America, Paintings and Sculpture.* New York, 1970.

HUNTINGTON, DAVID C. *The Landscapes of Frederic Edwin Church.* New York, 1966.

KENYON, PAUL. "Famous Gloucester Artist Finally Gets a Headstone," *Gloucester Daily Times,* June 3, 1960.

LOCHHEIM, ALINE B. "Forgotten Men of American Art," *The New York Times Magazine*, September 30, 1951, pp. 20–23.

M. and M. Karolik Collection of American Paintings, 1815 to 1865. Cambridge, 1949. (Published for the Museum of Fine Arts, Boston.) Introduction, "Trends in American Painting, 1815 to 1865," by JOHN I. H. BAUR.

M. and M. Karolik Collection of American Water Colors and Drawings, 1800–1875. 2 vols. Boston, 1962.

M. and M. Karolik Collection of Eighteenth-Century American Arts, Cambridge, 1941. (Published for the Museum of Fine Arts, Boston.)

McCORMICK, GENE E. "Fitz Hugh Lane, Gloucester Artist, 1804–1865." Unpublished master's thesis, Yale University, 1951.

———. "Fitz Hugh Lane, Gloucester Artist, 1804–1865," *Art Quarterly* 15 (Winter, 1952): 291–306.

McLANATHAN, RICHARD B. K. *Fitz Hugh Lane*. Boston, 1956. (Museum of Fine Arts Picture Book No. 8.)

MELLON, GERTRUD A., coordinating ed., and ELIZABETH A. WILDER, ed. *Maine and Its Role in American Art*. New York, 1963 (under the auspices of Colby College, Waterville, Maine).

Memorial of the Celebration of the Two Hundred and Fiftieth Anniversary of the Incorporation of the Town of Gloucester, Mass., August, 1892. Boston, 1901.

Nineteenth Century American Paintings, 1815–1865: From the Collection of Maxim Karolik; A Loan Exhibition to Mid-Western Museums. Minneapolis Institute of Arts, April 2–May 31, 1953.

Nineteenth Century American Paintings, 1815–1865: From the Private Collection of Maxim Karolik. Circulated by the Smithsonian Institution, 1954–1955–1956. Foreword by OTTO WHITMAN, JR.

NOVAK, BARBARA. *American Painting of the Nineteenth Century*. New York, 1969.

PARKER, BARBARA N. "American Paintings 1815–1865 in the M. and M. Karolik Collection," *Antiques* 60 (October, 1951): 292–96.

PETERS, HARRY T. *America on Stone*. New York, 1931.

Portfolio of the Old Print Shop, New York 1 (April, 1942): 9–13.

PRINGLE, JAMES R. *History of the Town and City of Gloucester, Cape Ann, Massachusetts*. Gloucester, Mass., 1892.

SHARF, FREDERIC A. "Fitz Hugh Lane: Visits to the Maine Coast, 1848–1855," Essex Institute *Historical Collections* 98 (April, 1962): 111–20.

———. "Fitz Hugh Lane, His Life and His Art," *Antiques* 78 (November, 1960): 452–55.

———. "Fitz Hugh Lane Reconsidered," Essex Institute *Historical Collections* 96 (January, 1960): 73–83.

STEBBINS, THEODORE E., JR. *Luminous Landscape: The American Study of Light, 1860–1875* (catalogue). Fogg Art Museum, Harvard University, Cambridge, Mass., April 18–May 11, 1966.

———. *Martin Johnson Heade* (catalogue). Whitney Museum *et al.,* New York, 1969.

TIBBETS, FREDERICK W. *The Story of Gloucester, Massachusetts*. (Address before the Convention of the Massachusetts State Firemen's Association at City Hall, Gloucester, 21 September 1916.) Gloucester, 1917.

WILMERDING, JOHN. "As Under a Bell Jar: A Study of Quality in Fitz Hugh Lane," *Antiques* 82 (October, 1962): 406–9.

———. *Fitz Hugh Lane: The First Major Exhibition* (catalogue). DeCordova Museum, Lincoln, Mass., and Colby College Art Museum, Waterville, Me., March–June, 1966.

———. *Fitz Hugh Lane, 1804–1865, American Marine Painter,* Salem, 1964.

———. "Fitz Hugh Lane, 1804–1865, American Marine Painter," Essex Institute *Historical Collections* 99 (July, 1963): 173–202, and 99 (October, 1963): 289–310.

———. "Fitz Hugh Lane, Painter of Gloucester," *Journey Through New England* 3 (1966): 72–74.

———. "Fitz Hugh Lane's Paintings Down East," *Down East* 12 (April, 1966): 22–25, 43.

———. *A History of American Marine Painting.* Boston and Toronto, 1968.

———. "Interpretations of Place: Views of Gloucester, Massachusetts, by American Artists," Essex Institute *Historical Collections* 103 (January, 1967), 53–65.

———. "The Lithographs of Fitz Hugh Lane," *Old-Time New England* 54 (Fall, 1963), 33–39.

———. *Pittura americana dell 'Ottocento.* Milan, 1969.

———. "Rediscovery: Fitz Hugh Lane," *Art in America* 53 (February, 1965): 62–69.

———. *Robert Salmon, Painter of Ship and Shore.* Boston, 1971.

———. *A Selection of Marine Paintings by Fitz Hugh Lane, 1804–1865.* Pictorial Supplement VII, *American Neptune,* Salem, Mass., 1965.

INDEX